17.50

80-1070

PR
3588
M475   Milton and the art
        of sacred song

DATE		JUN	2004
		JUN 09	
		JUL X X 2015	

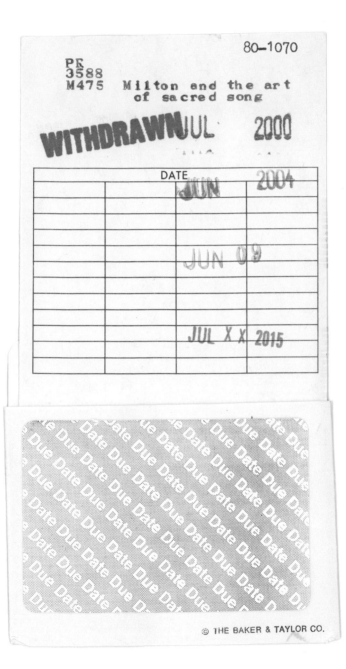

© THE BAKER & TAYLOR CO.

Milton & the Art of Sacred Song

ESSAYS BY
MORTIMER H. FRANK
VIRGINIA R. MOLLENKOTT
WILLIAM A. ORAM
J. MAX PATRICK
STELLA P. REVARD
JOHN T. SHAWCROSS
JAMES H. SIMS
ROGER H. SUNDELL

MILTON AND THE ART OF SACRED SONG

Edited by
J. Max Patrick & Roger H. Sundell

THE UNIVERSITY OF WISCONSIN PRESS

Published 1979

The University of Wisconsin Press
114 North Murray Street
Madison, Wisconsin 53715

The University of Wisconsin Press, Ltd.
1 Gower Street
London WC1E 6HA, England

Copyright © 1979
The Board of Regents of the University of Wisconsin System
All rights reserved

First printing

Printed in the United States of America

For LC CIP information see the colophon

ISBN 0-299-07830-2

IN MEMORY OF

Merritt Y. Hughes

Contents

"the hidden soul of harmony"

"Subject for Heroic Song"

Introduction

In the variety of their themes, the essays in this volume respond to the multifaceted nature of Milton's genius. They range over his knowledge of biblical, classical, and early Renaissance literature, his interest in music, his fascination with what is properly "heroic," and his artistry itself, in both general and special aspects. They are grouped according to such topics. But because one topic—Milton's lifelong dedication to sacred song—is recurrent throughout the essays, we have arranged them to emphasize the central significance of this unifying theme.

These essays are also tercentenary tributes to Milton, developed from papers presented in 1974 at conferences sponsored by the Wisconsin-Milwaukee, Marquette, and Wisconsin-Parkside Universities. In their revised, expanded, and updated form they constitute a selective harvest of what was sowed, weeded, and cultivated in those conferences. And they also provide memorial testimonies to Merritt Y. Hughes and grateful evidence of how his influence continues to inspire Miltonic scholarship not only in Wisconsin but throughout the learned world.

The collection makes available a fresh, representative, and timely body of literary scholarship focused upon Milton's poetry, especially as it reveals its author's tendency to draw inspiration from sacred writings and then to compose his own sacred poetic music in the service of his Creator. The opening essays by James H. Sims and Virginia R. Mollenkott thus probe Milton's literary uses of scriptural and apocryphal writings and suggest answers to the question, *Precisely how did Milton seek and discover poetic inspiration in what he believed to be the most sacred of textual sources available to fallen man?* The two essays that follow, by

William A. Oram and Roger H. Sundell, explore, first in the earlier poems and then in *Paradise Lost,* that process through which poetic inspiration is first conceptualized and articulated (in such figures as the genius or the muse), and then discovered to be a force in sacred song with a life of its own. The next two essays, by Mortimer H. Frank and J. Max Patrick, speculate on different aspects of the art of sacred song, first the nature and extent of its purely musical inheritance, and second the changing attitude of the poet-singer towards one of the most musical of poetic elements, rime. Finally, Stella P. Revard and John T. Shawcross address the oldest of questions about Milton's epic achievement in *Paradise Lost: Where in the poem does Milton locate those heroic qualities he chose to celebrate in "Heroic Song"?*

The heroic qualities Milton exalted were Christian ones, based on his interpretation of the New Testament. Undoubtedly the Bible was the principal source of his literary inspiration. That very fact gives rise to a problem raised by the essays in this volume: was Milton's use of the Bible more literary than doctrinal and didactic? Certainly, the influence of the Bible is pervasive in his works from the early psalm translations to *Paradise Regained* and *Samson Agonistes,* and in his prose from the Prolusions and the Commonplace Book to his last tract, *Of True Religion.* But contrary to appearances, that influence was not dominant. The Scriptures serve him as an adjunct, a springboard, and an initial source of inspiration. "On the Morning of Christ's Nativity" celebrates a major biblical event and refers to the Virgin, the manger, the three Wise Men, the shepherds, and the angel choir; and it works in some allusions to other parts of the Bible than the Gospel narratives of the birth of Jesus. But these biblical references are almost incidental, especially in the "Hymn." Pagan, classical, and mythological content bulks far larger: Nature ceases to wanton with her paramour, the Sun; meek-eyed Peace slides down with her myrtle wand; "Birds of Calm sit brooding on the charmed wave"; the music of the spheres rings out; there are references to the Saturnian age of gold and a return of Astraea to the world; with more imaginative than biblical basis, the "old Dragon," Satan, "wroth to see his Kingdom fail, / Swinges the scaly Horror of his folded tail"; and some seven stanzas are devoted to the departure of the pagan gods. Clearly, this is a work of inspired imagination and erudition that owes more to theology, mythology, and classical culture than to the Bible. The same is true of the fragment entitled "The Passion," where scriptural references are almost overwhelmed by Milton's comments on his own singing and by allusions to Hercules, Phoebus, and Cremona's Trump; the poem does not even reach its promised biblical theme, Jesus's sufferings and crucifixion. *L'Allegro* and *Il Penseroso* are obviously unscriptural songs. The gods and nymphs in *Arcades* are all pagan. Although *Comus* may have Christian implications of the kind pointed out by A. S. P. Woodhouse, its overt references and tone are classical and largely pagan. "Upon the Circumcision" is theological but only obliquely biblical. *Lycidas* contains scriptural references to "The Pilot of the *Galilean* lake," "the two-handed engine," an Angel, "the blest Kingdoms meek of joy and love," and "all the Saints above," but most of it is composed in classical terms as the pastoral song of the "uncouth Swain." The sonnets "Lady that in the prime of earliest youth," "Avenge, O Lord, thy slaughter'd Saints," and "When I consider how my light is spent" are so rich in biblical allusions that they may be regarded as biblical poems; but most of the other sonnets, including "Methought I saw my late espoused Saint," only partially qualify for that label.

References to the Bible are profuse and intricate in *Paradise Lost,* and its plot is ultimately Bible-based. Nevertheless, it is quite unlike what might be called "standard" seventeenth-century scriptural poems, versified condensations or paraphrases of the Bible such as Francis Quarles's *Divine Poems* based on Jonah, Esther, Job, Samson, and Ecclesiastes; Zachary Boyd's *Spiritual Songs: Or Holy Poems;* and Thomas Ellwood's somewhat later *Davideis.* Most of *Paradise Lost* is a product of Milton's own genius. While inspired by the Bible, it is built chiefly on scriptural exegesis, theology, mythology, Hebraic-Christian traditions, and the imaginings of the poet himself. In Books I and II, for example, the description of the falling of the defeated angels, their revival in Hell and their speeches and actions there, the identification of the pagan gods that Satan's followers became, his passage through Hell's gates, the personified abstractions Sin and Death, and Satan's voyaging through space owe much to poetic inspiration and very little to the Bible itself. The third book's conversations in

Heaven involve some Bible-based theology; but the account of Satan's journey to our earth and his adventures on the way owe almost nothing to Scriptures. The same holds for Book IV's account of Satan's discovering Eden, his spying on Adam and Eve, Uriel's identifying him, the dialogues of Adam and Eve, and Satan's temporary retreat from Eden. Parts of later books, such as Raphael's account of the Creation, depend more on the Bible, but even they go far beyond it with details invented by Milton or taken over from extrabiblical sources. Almost everything else that Raphael relates (including the long account of the battle in Heaven) and almost everything that Adam and Eve say to each other are Miltonic additions. To put it simply, the actual Scripture-derived content of *Paradise Lost* is not large; most of it is made up by the inspired poet or imaginatively reconstructed from extrabiblical sources. Regardless of whether the scriptural content of the "Heroic Song" is believed to be true, it is largely the work of a writer gifted in the art of invention.

It is the same with *Samson Agonistes*. The Bible says nothing about Samson's last day before he is taken to the Philistine temple. The visits to Samson by the Chorus, Manoa, Dalila, Harapha, and the Philistine officer are totally invented by Milton, as is most of the content of their speeches except for some information about earlier events, derived from the Bible but often embellished or rearranged or even telescoped. Milton's additions to the story, such as Samson's marrying Dalila and the invention of Harapha, are as free as his apparently deliberate failure to mention that Samson had served Israel for years as a Judge. In Milton's play, the Philistines are comparatively lenient: they allow Samson days of leisure when it is his "wont to sit" outside the mill in the fresh air, and, instead of forcibly hauling him to the Temple, they allow him to answer their urging with "I cannot come" and "I will not come" and only later threaten to drag him there if he will not agree to come. By that time some "rousing motions" within him have changed his mind: but those "motions" have no scriptural basis. Thus most of *Samson Agonistes,* though inspired by somewhat freely interpreted Scriptures, consists of speeches and encounters that are almost totally invented by the poet.

Paradise Regained is an exception, being more directly based on Holy Scriptures. But its very unusualness in this respect makes all the more apparent the fact that in most of his verse Milton embellished upon the Bible and used it as a source of inspiration for his own creative efforts. (Even in *Paradise Regained* the speeches in the dialogues between Jesus and Satan are inventive expansions upon the biblical sources; and the diabolic council is largely a product of Milton's imagination influenced by extrabiblical sources.) Accordingly, it is probably best to approach Milton's religious poetry as highly imaginative and speculative, not as biblically factual or doctrinal literature, and to regard it as literature intended less to instruct his readers and to close their minds by solving problems than to provide aesthetic pleasure, to promote thought, and to induce fertile discussions. He was not, like the Presbyterians of his day, saying, 'Here is the settled truth which you must accept as authoritative and established,' but, in effect, recommending, 'Think for yourself. I sing not to indoctrinate but to advance the discovery of truth by inspiring cooperative progressive interpretation of what God has revealed to man.'

In the prologue to Book III of *Paradise Lost,* the blind bard declares that he is "Smit with the love of sacred Song," that he visits Sion nightly, and that he then feeds on "thoughts, that voluntary move / Harmonious numbers." The passage describes a creative process Milton himself may well have experienced. Inspired by classical and other literatures, but chiefly by the Holy Bible, the poet creates his sacred song with its own great argument, its own answerable style, and its own distinct purpose of inspiring in a fit audience a love of beauty and a willingness to pursue truth.

"the Book of God before thee set"

Milton, *Literature as a Bible,*
and the Bible as Literature

JAMES H. SIMS

C. S. Lewis once remarked that the Bible is "not merely a sacred book but a book so remorselessly and continuously sacred that it does not invite, it excludes or repels, the merely aesthetic approach." He went on to say, "I cannot help suspecting . . . that those who read the Bible as literature do not read the Bible."[1] But as the context of his remarks shows Lewis did allow for the reading of the Bible for literary delight among Christians, though he thinks it is done only as a *tour de force* and with such delight coming only as a by-product of their search for religious meaning. People who read the Bible as literature do, however, read the Bible, and the lineage of their tribe extends far into the distant past. Although Lewis identifies the phrase "the Bible as literature" as a coinage of our age, it began to appear soon after Bishop Robert Lowth's *De sacra poesi Hebraeorum* was published in 1758;[2] and the literary approach to the Bible is implicit in the

I acknowledge with gratitude the gracious assistance of the Director and staff of the Henry E. Huntington Library and Art Gallery during my term as Reader there in 1973 and the financial aid granted by the Office of Research Administration of the University of Oklahoma towards the completion of this study.

1. "The Literary Impact of the Authorized Version," in *Selected Literary Essays,* ed. Walter Hooper (Cambridge, 1969), pp. 144, 142.

2. The earlier sense of "literature" as "instructed in the arts and letters" or the humanities is current from the late fifteenth through the sixteenth century, but it is obsolete by the time of Todd and Johnson (see *OED,* "Literature"). When Robert Lowth's *Lectures on the Sacred Poetry of the Hebrews* was published in an annotated translation in 1829, the editor, Calvin E. Stowe, preferred the phrase "the literature of the Bible" (p. xvi), though he referred more than once to the Bible as "a department of literature" (pp. v, xvi) and once to

biblical studies of Eusebius and Basil from the fourth century and explicit from the time that Ambrose's classical sermons converted Augustine from Manichaeism but not from rhetoric. As one seventeenth-century apologist for divine poetry put it, the English poet should transmute the Bible into poetry

> That they who take these Poems up as men,
> May lay them down as Saints made by his pen.
>   Thus *Ambrose* catch't an *Austin*[;] by his quaint
>   Divinity, the Manichee turn'd Saint.[3]

It may be granted that there are believers whose study of the Bible is almost exclusively devotional or doctrinal, but even many of them see an aesthetic approach as an aid to understanding—and consequently to faith and morals. It has long been so. From the seventh through the thirteenth centuries such commentators as Cassiodorus, Alain de Lille, Isidore of Seville, the Venerable Bede, Jonah Ibn Janah, and Ulrich showed their appreciation of the parallelism, tropes, and metaphors of the Bible's poetry and their admiration of the rhetorical excellence of its orations and exhortations as well as the simplicity and perspicuity of its narratives—and even such pre-Reformation writers drew no sharp line of distinction between the Bible and the secular literature of the Greek, Roman, and Arab worlds in their discussion of literary matters. To them the Bible, while unique in its claim to definitive revelation, shared much with all great literature in its technical devices and its generic distinctions, including its maintenance of decorum within those kinds.[4]

It is well known that Luther and Calvin led the Reformers in focusing strongly on the priority of the literal meaning of the text even, in Calvin's case, when such a focus meant rejecting as typical of Christ the "seed of the woman" in Genesis 3:15, or even, in Luther's case, when it meant admitting the existence of contra-

---

"the Bible . . . as a work of taste" (p. iv). John David Michaelis, the German scholar who translated, corrected, and refined Lowth's lectures, thereby launching (according to Stowe) "higher criticism," is called the "Patriarch of Sacred Literature" (pp. x–xi).

3. Thomas Washbourne, *Divine Poems* (London, 1654); the quoted lines are by "E. P.," and appear in the prefatory material following the title page. Typography is modernized in quotations from books printed in the sixteenth and seventeenth centuries.

4. Martin J. Buss, "The Study of Forms: Genre Consideration in Early and Medieval Biblical Studies," in *Old Testament Form Criticism*, ed. John H. Hayes (San Antonio, 1974), pp. 10–17.

dictory passages between, or even within, books of the Bible.[5] Yet both Luther and Calvin were remarkably free in their use of principles that centuries later would come to characterize "higher criticism," including a literary interest in genres, an early harbinger of "form criticism." Philip Melancthon and his student Matthias Flacius carried Luther's critical principles much further. In *Clavis Scripturae,* 1567, Flacius agrees that faith and moral commitment are basic requisites to an understanding of Scripture, but he adds the requirements of sensitivity to dialectic and rhetoric and of close attention to the *skopos,* or aim, which gives unity to the work (an emphasis borrowed from the Neoplatonic exegetes of Alexandria and Antioch). In other words, considerations of genre and decorum could be ignored only at the risk of misunderstanding a given particular passage.

Doubtless many people, perhaps some reading these words even now, agree with C. S. Lewis that the Bible is one of two things but not both: it is either a sacred book destined to live on in that exclusive capacity with perhaps a modicum of "literary enjoyment as a by-product"; or it is a collection of some good and some poor literature which will, as Christianity fades away, "follow the classics . . . into the ghost-life of the museum and the specialist's study."[6] Milton would, I submit, like most of his Christian humanist contemporaries, deny that the devotional and the literary approaches are polar extremes, for his comments, and even more clearly his practice, indicate that both ways of reading the Bible are equally durable, reciprocally related, and necessarily applicable to all literature—though fit readers who apply both belief and appreciation to

> What the sage Poets taught by th' heav'nly Muse
> Storied of old in high immortal verse
> (*A Mask*, 515–16)[7]

are in any age relatively few, for "unbelief is blind" (519).

Furthermore the Bible was for Milton considerably more than

5. G. Ernest Wright, "Historical Knowledge and Revelation," in *Translating and Understanding the Old Testament,* ed. H. T. Frank and W. L. Reed (Nashville, 1970), pp. 283–84.

6. Lewis, "Literary Impact," p. 145.

7. Quotations from Milton's poetry are taken from John Milton, *Complete Poems and Major Prose,* ed. Merritt Y. Hughes (New York, 1957).

the sole literal record of God's truth revealed to men. His awareness of problems concerning the copying of biblical manuscripts and the transmission of texts was, like Luther's and Calvin's, far more sophisticated than many of his modern readers realize. And Milton's conception of permissible methods of interpretation, largely as a result of his concern with genre and decorum and of his emphasis on the "internal scripture of the Holy Spirit . . . engraved upon the hearts of believers," was much broader than some scholars think. In *Christian Doctrine* Milton says,

The external scripture, particularly the New Testament, has often been liable to corruption and is, in fact, corrupt. This has come about because it has been committed to the care of various untrustworthy authorities, has been collected together from an assortment of divergent manuscripts, and has survived in a medley of transcripts and editions . . . I do not know why God's providence should have committed the contents of the New Testament to such wayward and uncertain guardians, unless it was so that this very fact might convince us that the Spirit which is given to us is a more certain guide than scripture, and that we ought to follow it.

(*CPW*, VI, 587–89)[8]

Jesus speaks in *Paradise Regained* about the necessity of bringing "A spirit and judgment equal or superior" to what one reads, and this is true even of the reader of the external Scripture and not simply of the reader of classical literature. And the man who brings such a spirit to his reading need not be overly fastidious about what he reads. That Milton read the Bible as literature means, among other things, that he read it for delight as well as for instruction and that he regarded it as also a source of literature. Indeed the Bible is a specimen of the genus literature; though initially the product of uniquely inspired men, it has come to depend largely on the special sensitivity of its reader in order to communicate its truth. In this sense it is of the family of literature. Milton saw even extrabiblical literature, particularly classical literature, as a kind of secular Bible from which the spiritual man, indwelt by the incorruptible Spirit, might draw beneficial doctrine, for God had communicated truth through especially gifted

8. Quotations from Milton's prose are taken from the Yale edition (*CPW*): *Complete Prose Works of John Milton,* ed. Don M. Wolfe et al. (New Haven, 1953–).

men of all ages. The abilities required for the "very critical art of composition," Milton says in *The Reason of Church Government,*

wheresoever they be found, are the inspired guift of God, rarely bestow'd, but yet to some (though most abuse) in every Nation: and are of power beside the office of a pulpit, to imbreed and cherish in a great people the seeds of vertu and publick civility . . .

(*CPW,* I, 816)

In *Areopagitica* Milton argues against licensing because the licensors might delete "one sentence of a ventrous edge, utter'd in the height of zeal, and who knows whether it might not be the dictat of a divine Spirit [?]" (*CPW,* II, 534). He has in mind Christian writers, or at worst, heretics (in his mild sense of those who hold an opinion different from the majority). But that a divine spirit may have inspired pagan writers is implicit in his argument, also in *Areopagitica,* that if truth is confined or bound, "she turns herself into all shapes, except her own," and appears like falsehood (563). Therefore the attempt to defend and protect truth by severely restricting the channels through which it may come to man is self-defeating, for "Truth is compar'd in Scripture to a streaming fountain" whose waters must be allowed to flow freely (543).

Literature, then, in the most inclusive sense—encompassing all the branches of learning represented in the reading program outlined in *Of Education*—constitutes a secular Bible. It is incomplete and obscure, even misleading to one without the advantage of comparison with the external Scripture or guidance from the internal Scripture; yet it is spiritually beneficial for the sincere, truth-seeking conscience. As Milton points out both in *Areopagitica* and in the prefatory epistle to *Samson Agonistes,* Paul included quotations from pagan poets in his New Testament epistles.[9] The passage in *Areopagitica* is of special interest, for

9. "The Apostle *Paul* himself thought it not unworthy to insert a verse of *Euripides* into the Text of Holy Scripture, I Cor. xv. 33" ("Of that sort of Dramatic Poem which is call'd Tragedy," *Samson Agonistes,* in *Complete Poems,* ed. Hughes, p. 549)). Richard Francis Weymouth (*The New Testament in Modern Speech,* 5th ed. [Boston, 1943], pp. 674, 690) identifies the following sources for some of Paul's quotations of secular literature: Epimenides, sixth-century B.C. poet-prophet of Crete, Acts 17:28 and Titus 1:12; Seneca, Acts 17:24, Romans 7:23, I Corinthians 9:25 and 12:27, II Corinthians 3:17 and 12:15, and Ephesians 6:12. Weymouth does not annotate I Corinthians 15:33, though he encloses it in quotation marks.

Milton strongly asserts that much good is obtainable from extrabiblical literature and presents as examples Moses and Daniel
as well as Paul. Good Christians, says Milton, profit by reading
"books of all sorts" (508); indeed Christians forbidden the use of
heathen learning in Julian the Apostate's time considered such a
deprivation more damaging to the church's faith and progress
than the cruel persecutions of Diocletian. St. Basil had pointed out
the spiritual uses of Homer's mock-heroic *Margites;* "why not then
of *Morgante,* an Italian Romanze[?]" (510–11). Had not the great
Selden proven that "all opinions, yea errors known, read, and
collated, are of main service & assistance toward the speedy
attainment of what is truest"? (513). It is in such a context that
Milton dares to elevate "our sage and serious Poet Spencer" above
Scotus or Aquinas as a teacher because he shows Guion's virtue of
temperance being proved "by what is contrary" (515–16). In this
Spenser is like the Bible, which "oftimes relates blasphemy not
nicely, . . . describes the carnall sense of wicked men not
unelegantly, . . . brings in holiest men passionately murmuring
against providence through all the arguments of *Epicurus*" (517).
Though the surface argument here involves "knowing good by
evil," Milton is making clear through his examples that not
everything in the Bible is good, nor is everything in extrabiblical
literature evil. The best and truest, then, is arrived at through a
kind of reciprocating relationship between the Bible and pagan
literature, and the "true warfaring Christian" is as handicapped by
the lack of other books to read as he is by the lack of trial to prove
his virtue.

   Milton's use of the case of Dionysius Alexandrinus clarifies the
point. A presbyter's questioning of Dionysius's practice of
studying heretical and heathen works threw him into a crisis of
conscience. The crisis was resolved by a vision in which God
assured Dionysius of his sufficiency "both to judge aright, and to
examine each matter" for himself (511). Dionysius returned to his
habit of promiscuous reading for he found the vision corroborated
in Paul's advice to the Thessalonians: "Prove all things, hold fast
that which is good" (511–12; I Thess. 5:21). Two important
principles emerge from this example. First, because the believer
has the Spirit of God and his own conscience to guide his

judgment, God "trusts him with the gift of reason to be his own chooser" (514); second, the reading of pagan or heretical books yields positively good and true precepts and examples which the Christian should hold fast and observe. Milton had earlier declared in his *Apology for Smectymnuus* that pagan love poets and fanciful romancers who had to "many others . . . bin the fuell of wantonnesse and loose living" had to him "by divine indulgence prov'd . . . so many incitements . . . to the love and stedfast observation of . . . virtue" (*CPW*, I, 891). But in *Areopagitica* he has advanced beyond such negative examples to assert the positive benefits of pagan literature.

Paradise Regained demonstrates through Jesus himself the virtuous uses of nonbiblical writings. Jesus parries Satan's arguments with knowledge drawn from classical history, literature, and philosophy. And when he rejects Satan's offer of power through the learning of Athens, his scorn is directed at Satan's suggestion that he achieve God's purposes through Satanic means and according to Satanic timing, not indiscriminately at all extrabiblical learning. Recall in that famous rejection speech the following enigmatic lines:

> Think not but that I know these things; or think
> I know them not; not therefore am I short
> Of knowing what I ought: he who receives
> Light from above, from the fountain of light,
> No other doctrine needs, though granted true;
> But these are false, or little else but dreams,
> Conjectures, fancies, built on nothing firm.
>   (*PR* IV.286–92)

That Jesus does "know these things" has been shown by his earlier references to the Oracle at Delphos (I.458), to Quintius and other poor men who had performed mighty deeds without monetary reward (II.446), and to Socrates (III.96). But even if he knew them not, he is not deficient in needful knowledge, for he has light from God's Spirit and from the Bible. If a man lacks the "Light from above," however, the "dreams" of pagan literature, though not firmly grounded, may direct him towards the light; for some of the doctrine of mythology may be granted to be true. As for piety, the epitome of song is found in the Psalms, inspired by God, not by Satan. Yet there are pagan poems

> where moral virtue is express'd
> By light of Nature, not in all quite lost.
> (PR IV.351–52)

Jesus's rejection of classical literature, then, is made from the secure position of one who has God's revelation in the Bible and God's indwelling Spirit to guide him to truth. Of one not in such a position Jesus can confidently say,

> who reads
> Incessantly, and to his reading brings not
> A spirit and judgment equal or superior,
> (And what he brings, what needs he elsewhere seek)
> Uncertain and unsettl'd still remains,
> Deep verst in books and shallow in himself.
> (PR IV.322–27)

But a loophole is deliberately left for the man who, though he has no "Light from above," has "A spirit and judgment equal or superior" to what he reads. A dream that may be granted true, though based on nothing firm, is preferable to no dream at all; it may lead towards a glimpse, however dim, of the hem of Truth's garment, even if the dreamer cannot reach out and touch it. The reader who brings the requisite spirit need not seek it elsewhere, but he who lacks such a spirit may, on the other hand, seek diligently for it, feeling keenly his ignorance of himself and of God, of

> how the world began, and how man fell
> Degraded by himself, on grace depending.
> (PR IV.310–12)

Indeed, as Anne Bowers Long says in her unpublished dissertation, "If a pagan proceeds in the process of regeneration through response to the imperfect law of nature, he may be able to use his reason, memories, and imagination to prophesy in mythology the significance of the covenant of grace."[10] Mrs. Long further in-

---

10. Anne Bowers Long, "The Relations Between Classical and Biblical Allusions in Milton's Later Poems" (Ph.D. diss., University of Illinois, 1967), p. 32.

terprets Milton's view of mythology in classical literature when she says:

Mythology, since it represents human efforts to understand the spirit of law by the law of nature in the heart without the guidance and imposition of external law, is closer to the Gospel dispensation than is the Mosaic law.[11]

By a process the reverse of that by which the Christian may see the spirit (not the letter) of biblical truth corroborated in analogous classical myth, the pagan may use his reason and imagination to make a prophetically spiritual use of his myths to anticipate elements of the New Testament story of redemption. Whether or not Mrs. Long is completely right in her interpretation, it is clear that, for Milton, allusions to classical literature are more than surface ornaments, even in *Paradise Regained*. The Christ who has alluded to classical myth himself and is associated with Hercules and Oedipus in the climactic scene of the poem surely does not mean his rejection of such literature to be absolute in any context other than the one in which he makes it.[12] And Milton's use of citations to pagan poets in *Christian Doctrine* in support of biblical doctrines, though negligible in number when compared with the biblical references, indicates that he considered—and expected at least some of his readers to consider—the world's great works of literature a source of truth to confirm revealed truth. Inferior to the canonical Scriptures such works are to Milton; yet interpreted spiritually they are treated as though superior even to the apocryphal books, which, he said, "are not admitted as evidence in deciding points of faith" (*CPW*, VI, 574), while Homer supports free will, Thucydides and Virgil piacular punishment, Ovid the nature of personal sin, and Homer's Penelope wifely decorum.[13] That classical myths in poetry and

---

11. Long, "Relations," p. 34.

12. See B. Rajan, "Jerusalem and Athens: The Temptation of Learning in *Paradise Regained*," in *Th' Upright Heart and Pure: Essays on John Milton Commemorating the Tercentary of the Publication of Paradise Lost*, ed. Amadeus P. Fiore (Pittsburgh, 1967), pp. 61–74.

13. In *Christian Doctrine* Milton reproves Christian interpreters who make the mistake of too slavishly following the letter of Scripture and thus putting the blame on God for reprobating hardhearted unbelievers whose hearts God himself is said to have hardened.

drama may guide the gentile conscience towards a spiritual circumcision is a conviction only a step removed from the implications of Paul's rhetorical questions: "If the uncircumcision
keep the righteousness of the law, shall not his uncircumcision be
counted for circumcision? And shall not uncircumcision which is
by nature, if it fulfil the law, judge thee who by the letter and
circumcision dost transgress the law?" (Rom. 2:26–27).[14] And
Milton's position is consistent with Paul's conclusion that "he *is* a
Jew, which is one inwardly; and circumcision *is that* of the heart,
in the spirit, *and* not in the letter; whose praise *is* not of men, but
of God" (Rom. 2:29).

If pagan works contain truth sufficient to corroborate, even if
only in an analogous and illustrative way, biblical teachings that
correspond with the light of nature, and if they may be beneficial
in leading the heathen towards the true spiritual light of the
gospel, how much more may they help guide the Christian—Paul,
his audience, even Christ in the wilderness—who has the internal
Scripture to guide him in separating wheat from chaff? And in
how much greater measure may the imaginative works of
Christian poets like Tasso and Spenser serve as an extension or
extrapolation of the external Word through the operation of the
Spirit in their composing and our reading of their literary works?
If, Milton maintains in *Eikonoklastes,* God

left our affections to be guided by his sanctifying spirit, so did he likewise
our words to be put into us without our premeditation; not onely those
cautious words to be us'd before Gentiles and Tyrants, but much more
those filial words, of which we have so frequent use in our access with
freedom of speech to the Throne of Grace.

(*CPW,* III, 506)

Such interpreters, says Milton, "even a heathen like Homer emphatically reproves . . . in
Odyssey, I. 7:

> They perish by their own impieties.

—and again, through the mouth of Jupiter, I. 32:

> O how falsly men
> Accuse us Gods as authors of their ill,
> When by the bane their owne bad lives instill
> They suffer all the miseries of their states—
> Past our inflictions and beyond their fates."
> (*CPW,* VI, 202; cf. II, 294)

Other examples referred to in the text above appear in *CPW,* VI, 387, 388, 728.

14. References to Scripture conform to the King James Version.

And if the Spirit guides in unpremeditated prayers may he not guide as well in "unpremeditated Verse," particularly for a Christian who engages in

devout prayer to that eternall Spirit who can enrich with all utterance and knowledge, and sends out his Seraphim with the hallow'd fire of his Altar to touch and purify the lips of whom he pleases [?]

(*CPW*, I, 820–21)

Assuredly, Milton would say, he both may and does do so; and though all literature must be brought under the "determinant sentence" of canonical Scripture, all literature, including the Bible as a higher form of it, is the province of the poet—and most especially of the poet who has the advantage "over and above of being a Christian" (CPW, I, 812).

It is clear from his *Of Education* that the Bible is only one, though a supremely important one, of the many books to be used "to repair the ruins of our first parents by regaining to know God aright" (*CPW*, II, 366–67). The knowledge of God and things invisible depends on "the orderly conning over the visible and inferior creature" and since these "sensible things" are described best in no single language, the study of "the languages of those people . . . most industrious after wisdom" (368–69) is of first priority; and among these the first is Latin. The earliest daytime readings and lectures are to be in grammar, moral education, arithmetic, and geometry, while the evenings are to be "taken up in the easie grounds of Religion, and the story of Scripture" (387). In the next stage, days are devoted to agriculture, geography, natural philosophy, "physic," and poetry and moral philosophy in Greek and Latin; evenings are given to bringing the day's studies "under the determinant sentence of *David,* or *Salomon,* or the Evangels and *Apostolic* scriptures" (397). By the time politics and oratory are central in the next form, Hebrew should have been mastered "that the Scriptures may be now read in their own originall" (400). Finally the students are ready for logic, rhetoric, and poetics so that they may prepare to write, speak, and compose "in every excellent matter" (406). Milton expects the Bible to be fully as instrumental as the Greek, Latin, and Italian writers in causing the young men to see the inferiority of "our common rimers and play-writes" (405) and to recognize "what Religious, what glorious and magnificent use might be made of Poetry both in divine and humane things" (405–6). The Bible, then, is included not only for moral and doctrinal instruction; it is also literature, for its human authors are exemplary of good literary practice.

Two years before *Of Education* Milton had, in *The Reason of Church Government,* spoken of the Song of Solomon as "a divine pastoral Drama . . . consisting of two persons, and a double *Chorus,* as *Origen* rightly judges," and of the Apocalypse as "the majestick image of a high and stately tragedy" (*CPW,* I, 815).[15] He further said that "those frequent songs throughout the law and prophets . . . not in their divine argument alone, but in the very critical art of composition may be easily made appear over all the kinds of Lyrick poesy, to be incomparable" (816). Many years later Milton put similar praise for the Bible's poetry in the mouth of Jesus, with emphasis on its priority in time and its having been divinely inspired.

> All our Law and Story strew'd
> With Hymns, our Psalms with artful terms inscrib'd
> Our Hebrew Songs and Harps in *Babylon,*
> That pleas'd so well our Victors' ear, declare
> That rather *Greece* from us these Arts deriv'd;
> Ill imitated . . .
>
> (*PR* IV.334–39)

When allowance is made for the exaggeration and the unyielding tone called for in such a context as the temptation to bow down to Satan, the view Jesus expresses is similar to one voiced often in the sixteenth and seventeenth centuries: that the Bible contains the greatest poetic art. Many then went further to describe the Bible as, even in its prose parts, a rich source of material for divine poetry. That Milton agreed is obvious from his choice of subjects for his major poems; but the background against which that choice was made has been insufficiently surveyed.[16] Between the 1570s, say, and the 1650s, the argument in

15. See Barbara K. Lewalski, "*Samson Agonistes* and the 'Tragedy' of the Apocalypse," *PMLA* 85 (1970), 1050–62.

16. Lily B. Campbell (*Divine Poetry and Drama in Sixteenth-Century England* [London, 1959]) and Israel Baroway ("The Bible as Poetry in the English Renaissance," *Journal of English and Germanic Philology* 32 [1933], 447–80) have dealt with this background. I express in the text below my differences with Campbell's views. Baroway's contention that medieval allegorical rationalization was "without aesthetic intent, and indeed . . . often

favor of divine poetry changed little, but the theoretical basis for treating biblical subjects in the fashions and forms inspired by the classical muses—and for making liberal use of poetic invention as a means of expanding and interpreting the story rather than of ornamentation—shifted considerably. Sidney set the pattern for the discussion in his *Apology for Poetry* in 1580 and seventy-five years later Abraham Cowley, in his preface to the *Davideis* of 1656, gave utterance to the principle that the divine poet must be more than a translator or a versifier of English biblical prose. Though the Bible provides the best materials in the world for poetry, "None but a good *Artist* will know how to do it: neither must we think to cut and polish *Diamonds* with so little pains and skill as we do *Marble*."[17] Between Sidney and Cowley lie acres of diamonds of Scripture which are, in spite of imperfect cutting, given poetic settings in the continuing attempt to prove that divine poetry can replace secular poetry. Those who believe that divine and secular poetry are sister arts intended to benefit each other, like those who reject poetry of any kind, are in the minority.

I shall not attempt to retell the story here of this controversy over poetry, seen on the one hand as "the principall Authour of lyes" whose main aim is "to deceive mens mindes with the delectation of fables"[18] and on the other hand as the choicest medium of the Spirit of God who in those "sacred songs in Scripture" has shown that it will "breathe through what pipe it please."[19] Irreconcilable as these two views seem, they are based on the common premise that God breathed through chosen men who then wrote the books of the Bible as the Holy Spirit directed. But from this point the views diverge sharply. Those opposing the use of the human arts of poetry, painting, and music for divine subjects assume that these arts were originated by Satan and have been so hopelessly corrupted by the pagan sensuality they have served through the centuries that God and all good men instinctively abhor them as a means of praising God or instructing

anti-aesthetic in implication" and that the "Renaissance fashioned a new, vital conception of allegory which gave the Bible its poetic due" is not adequately supported within his essay.

17. Abraham Cowley, "The Preface," *Poems* (London, 1656).

18. Henry Cornelius Agrippa, *Of the Vanitie and Uncertaintie of Artes and Sciences: Englished by Ia. San.* [James Sanford] Gent. (London, 1575), p. 11.

19. Giles Fletcher, "To the Reader," *Christs Victorie and Triumph in Heaven And Earth, Over and After Death* (London, 1632).

men in God's truth. Those favoring divine poetry assume that
David, for instance, was an accomplished poet and a skilled
musician before God breathed the psalms through him; in short,
God chose to use human art as his vehicle for divine truth, for the
art was his gift in the first place. Francis Quarles satirizes the view
that human art is Satanic in *The Shepheards Oracles;* Canonicus
seeks to instruct the enthusiastic Anarchus:

> Canon. Let's try a Syllogisme; (Art infuses
> Spirit into the children of the Muses)
> Whereby stout error shall be forc'd to yield
> And Truth shall sit sole Mistresse of the field.

> Anar. Art me no Arts; that which the Spirit infuses
> Shall edge my tongue: what tell'st thou me of Muses;
> Those Pagan Gods; the Authours of your Schismes?
> Pish! tell not me of Arts, and *Silisismes;*
> I care not for your Quirks, and new devices
> Of studied wit: we use to play our prizes,
> With common weapons; and with downright knocks,
> We beat down Sin, and Error, like an Oxe.[20]

The view, however, that gentler arts inspired by the Muses may be
more effective in the service of scriptural truth was expressed in
George Ballard's invocation to his poetic version of the story of
Susanna:

> O thou that learnd'st old *Isay's* sonne to sing
> The songs of Sion tun'd on silver-string:
> (Great God of *Moses,* God of Muses too)
> Teach me to sing, as thou taught'st him to do.[21]

But the proponents of divine poetry needed a basis in
philosophy and theology for their advocacy of the Muses, as well
as of Moses, as inspirers of poetry. Professor Lily Campbell has
described the elevation of Urania as the Muse of Christian poetry
by Du Bartas and later poets, culminating in Milton's *Paradise
Lost,* but the dependence upon a Christian Muse of poetry is more
a symptom of the increasing acceptance of divine poetry than a
cause of it.[22] Not even the great Du Bartas' influence could have

20. London, 1646, p. 86.
21. George Ballard, "The Authour's Petition," *The History of Susanna* (London, 1638).
22. Campbell, *Divine Poetry,* pp. 87–92.

stilled some of the thoughtful objectors had not a prior assumption spread pervasively and cumulatively through the late sixteenth- and early seventeenth-century consciousness: the assumption that all great art, and literature in particular, is inspired in some sense, and that it constitutes an extracanonical "Bible" through which God obscurely revealed himself and his purposes preparatory to providing the clearer and more complete revelation of the Old and New Testaments.[23] Giles Fletcher gives eloquent voice to the commonplace idea that the obscure fables of the gentiles typify truths made clear by the Bible:

> Who doth not see drown'd in Deucalions name
> (When earth his men, and sea had lost his shore)
> Old Noah? And in Nisus lock the same
> Of Sampson yet alive? and long before
> In Phaethons, mine own fall I deplore:
> > But he that conquer'd hell, to fetch again
> > His virgin widow, by a serpent slain,
> Another Orpheus was then dreaming poets feigne:
>
> That taught the stones to melt for passion,
> And dormant sea, to heare him, silent lie;
> And at his voice, the watrie nation
> To flock, as if they deem'd it cheap, to buy
> With their own deaths his sacred harmonie:
> > The while the waves stood still to heare his song,
> > And steadie shore wav'd with the reeling throng
> Of thirsty souls, that hung upon his fluent tongue.[24]

The example of the Fletchers, not to mention Sandys, Drayton, Quarles, Sylvester, and many more, shows that while Lily Campbell is essentially correct in identifying Du Bartas' *L'Uranie* as the work that both "provided a Muse for Christian poetry" and

23. Long presents extended quotations from such Christian writers of diverse convictions on other subjects as William Prynne, John Goodwin, Arthur Golding, Sir Henry Reynolds, and George Sandys. She concludes that Milton's uses of biblical and classical allusion show him feeling much less ambivalence about the validity of myth than these other writers. "Where . . . other Puritans cite the remnant of the divine image in the hearts of men only to rob the unregenerate of any excuse for their unbelief, Milton considers that the remnant allows all to grow to belief; . . . it is the will of the unregenerate, not the inadequacy of their reason, which prevents their regeneration" ("Relations," p. 166). In *Christian Doctrine* Milton says: "Everyone is provided with a sufficient degree of innate reason for him to be able to resist evil desires by his own effort" (*CPW*, VI, 186).

24. Fletcher, *Christs Victorie*, pp. 50–51.

"gave unity and direction to the whole movement" in the sixteenth
century, she overstates some of the specific "tenets of the
movement . . . firmly established" by Du Bartas.[25] Such poets as I
have mentioned would have agreed that "poetry must be
reclaimed from the base uses to which it had been put," as Miss
Campbell says (80), but they would not have agreed that all
poetry had been so abased or that all nonsacred poetry has a
deleterious effect. They recognized poetry as a heavenly gift, but
did not reject, as Miss Campbell says they did, the idea that poetic
skill is partly the "result of study and learning."[26] Rather than to
insist that "Biblical story must be substituted for pagan
mythology" (80), these poets wished to fuse classical and biblical
material in order to impress upon the reader the universality of
moral and spiritual truths, as well as to exploit the typological
possibilities in myth. They agreed to a man that "better material
for poetry lies in the history of faith's effects than in old classical
stories" (80), but they saw the Bible as better not because it is the
antithesis of classical literature but because it constitutes a clear
and definitive fulfillment of truths only dimly perceived in that
literature's mythology.

Michael Drayton will serve as an example. More than one critic
has cited Drayton as a poet who views classical and biblical
literature as antithetical. Yet his famous statement in the preface
to A Heavenly Harmonie that he sang "not of Mars, the god of
Wars, nor of Venus, the goddesse of love, but of the Lord of
Hostes . . . Not of Vanitie, but of Veritie; not of Tales, but of
Truethes," should be considered in context. In the clause immediately preceding the series of opposites just quoted, Drayton
says to his readers, "(if thou shalt be the same in hart thou art in
name, I mean a Christian) I doubt not, but thou wilt take as great
delight in these, as in any Poetical fiction."[27] The Christian, then,
is assumed to be familiar with the tales of Mars and Venus and to

25. Campbell, Divine Poetry, p. 80.

26. Compare Milton's emphasis on "industrious and select reading, steddy observation,
insight into all seemly and generous arts and affaires" in addition to the inspiration of the
Spirit (Reason of Church Government, CPW, I, 821).

27. "To the curteous Reader," A Heavenly Harmonie of Spirituall Songes and holy
Himnes, of Godly Men, Patriarkes, and Prophets (London, 1610—originally printed in
1591). But see Campbell, Divine Poetry, p. 61, and Stanley Stewart, The Enclosed Garden:
The Tradition and the Image in Seventeenth-Century Poetry (Madison, 1966), p. 5.

take "as great delight" in biblical truths, not a greater delight. And though in the preface to his *Moyses in a Map of His Miracles* Drayton disclaimed the use of "any . . . habilments of invention or Poesie, should they seem never so delightfull," he surely expected the reader familiar with the classical and Renaissance *topos* of the *locus amoenus* to recognize the "habilments of . . . Poesie" in his highly conventional and completely nonbiblical description of Midian's babbling brooks, fragrant groves and fields, soft breezes, and warbling birds.[28]

The underlying principle of seeing truth even in these tales and verity in the apparent vanity of myth had been stated even before Sidney by Thomas Wilson.

The saiying of Poetes, and all their fables, are not to bee forgotten, for by them we maie talke at large, and win men by perswasion, if we declare before hand, that these tales wer not fained of soche wisemen without cause, neither yet continued untill this time, and kepte in memorie without good consideracion, and thereupon declare the true meaning of al soche writing. . . . The Poetes were wise men, and wished in harte the redresse of thinges . . . [;] thei did in colours paint them out, and told men by shadowes, what thei should doe in good sothe . . .[29]

It remained for Abraham Cowley—himself one who seems to set the Bible and classical literature in opposition to each other and yet actually fuses them through his use of allusions and classical forms, the Pindaric ode for example—to approve of divine poetry but to suggest that no one had yet successfully practiced it. His emphasis radically shifts the whole perspective from which the question of divine poetry versus secular poetry had been considered. Earlier proponents argue that the truth of the Bible can be communicated with a special charm and persuasiveness in poetry and still be faithful to the original text; Cowley argues that a true poet cannot be a mere translator, and the poet's task is to interpret and cast into new idioms and forms the "lost Excellencies of another *Language*."[30] "I am not so much enamoured of the *Name Translator,* as not to wish rather to be *Something Better,* though it want yet a *Name,*" he said; his aim in his version of Pindar, for

28. *Moyses in a Map of His Miracles* (London, 1604), preface and pp. 25–28.
29. "On Poetical Narration," in *The Arte of Rhetorique* (London, 1560—first published, 1553), fol. 99. ii.
30. Cowley, "Preface" to the "Pindarique Odes" in *Poems,* Sig. Aaa2.

example, was not so much "to let the Reader know precisely what [Pindar] spoke, as what was his *way* and *manner* of speaking."[31] His preface to his *Davideis* makes even clearer the "Idea" he had conceived of but felt inadequate to realize himself.

All the *Books* of the *Bible* are either already most admirable, and exalted pieces of *Poesie,* or are the best *Materials* in the world for it. Yet, though they be in themselves so proper to be made use of for this purpose; None but a good *Artist* will know how to do it: neither must we think to cut and polish *Diamonds* with so little pains and skill as we do *Marble.* For if any man design to compose a *Sacred Poem,* by onely turning a story of the *Scripture,* like Mr. *Quarles's,* or some other godly matter, like Mr. *Heywood of Angels,* into *Rhyme;* He is so far from elevating of *Poesie,* that he onely abases *Divinity.* In brief, he who can write a *prophane Poem well,* may write a *Divine one better;* but he who can do that but ill, will do this much worse. The same fertility of *Invention,* the same wisdom of *Disposition;* the same *Judgement* in observance of *Decencies,* the same lustre and vigor of *Elocution;* the same modesty and majestie of *Number;* briefly the same kinde of *Habit,* is required to both; only this latter allows better *stuff,* and therefore would look more deformedly, if *ill drest* in it. I am farre from assuming to my self to have fulfilled the duty of this weighty undertaking: But sure I am, that there is nothing yet in our *Language* (nor perhaps in *any*) that is in any degree answerable to the *Idea* that I conceive of it. And I shall be ambitious of no other fruit from this weak and imperfect attempt of mine, but the opening of a way to the courage and industry of some other persons, who may be better able to perform it throughly and successfully.[32]

Whether or not Cowley's words had any influence on Milton, within a few years after the *Davideis* Milton was engaged in composing a poem that would fulfill Cowley's "Idea" and transcend it as far as that idea surpassed the practice of divine rhymers like Sandys and Quarles, Ballard, Wishart, Washbourne, and Murford. When Milton published his major poems in 1667, 1671, and 1674, here was the "better stuff" of the Bible properly habited; and Milton had not only supplied the "lost Excellencies of another *Language* with new ones in" his own, he had transmuted the narratives of classical literature and of both Old and New Testaments into a transcendent myth that capsulized in an

---

31. Ibid.
32. Cowley, "The Preface," *Poems,* Sig. [(b)3ʳ⁻ᵛ].

intensely personal vision centuries of pagan, rabbinical, and patristic tradition. Milton does at times adhere quite closely to the literal text in his poetry; but more often he has, as is his practice with all his sources, made the sense clear in phrases distinctively his own. "It is not hard," he said, "for any man, who hath a Bible in his hands, to borrow good words and holy sayings in abundance; but to make them his own, is a work of grace onely from above."[33] *Paradise Lost, Paradise Regained,* and *Samson Agonistes* aim not to let the reader know exactly what the Bible says but rather to communicate a conception of the essential truth and the overriding tone of its message; Milton's narrator becomes a choric voice to express from a single perspective more than sixteen centuries of concern with literature as a Bible and with the Bible as literature.

33. *Eikonoklastes, CPW,* III, 553.

The Pervasive Influence
of the Apocrypha in
Milton's Thought and Art

VIRGINIA R. MOLLENKOTT

The Apocrypha, those books included in the Greek (Septuagint) and Latin (Vulgate) Christian Old Testament but excluded from the Hebrew Bible, exerted a pervasive influence on Milton and other Renaissance Christian humanists, an influence which has frequently remained unrecognized in modern scholarship. In *Milton's Use of Du Bartas,* for instance, George Coffin Taylor listed some sixty themes in *Paradise Lost* which were for the most part "the common property of Medieval and Renaissance writers" as a warning against attempting to trace these Miltonic themes to particular sources.[1] But although Taylor mentioned that many of these themes had been traced by Robbins to Greek and Latin commentaries on Genesis,[2] he did not draw the obvious conclusion that the commonplace themes of the Middle Ages and Renaissance are commonplace precisely because they are drawn from biblical literature, either canonical or apocryphal. In *Christian Doctrine* Milton insists that he adheres to the Holy Scriptures alone; and although he deviates from this policy for poetic details where Scripture is silent, he abides by it as much as possible not only for the establishment of doctrinal concepts but also for major poetic characters, places, and events.

1. Cambridge, Mass., 1934, pp. 15–23.
2. Frank Egleston Robbins, *The Hexaemeral Literature: A Study of the Greek and Latin Commentaries on Genesis* (Chicago, 1912).

It is therefore important that the student of Milton's sources turn first to the Canon and then to the Apocrypha before moving outward toward patristic, rabbinical, or classical areas.[3]

There are several reasons why the Apocrypha should be given preference in Milton studies over sources farther removed from the text of Scripture, such as patristic or rabbinical lore. First, it is usually wise to assume that an author makes use of familiar and easily accessible sources before he delves into more obscure ones—and the apocryphal books were bound into all English Bibles printed before 1629 and many thereafter,[4] including of course Milton's 1612 copy of the King James Version. Second, the close interrelationship between the Canon and the Apocrypha would cause Milton to respect its details as more authoritative than those of more secular authors; for instance, the 1560 Geneva Version, a copy of which Milton may have owned,[5] gives some ninety-seven marginal references to the New Testament in Ecclesiasticus and Wisdom of Solomon alone, and cites apocryphal books at least fifty-three times in the margins of the New Testament. Since these marginal citations indicate either significant parallels or the actual influence of the Apocrypha on New Testament authors, such testimony from the Calvinistic translators at Geneva could only make Milton feel it natural to turn to the Apocrypha when the Canon was either scanty or silent.[6] And the fact that the Anglican Church recognized the Apocrypha's value for reading "for example of life and in-struction of manners" would also tend to elevate this source above other extracanonical sources.

It has not been customary in Milton studies to make any clear-cut distinction between Canon and Apocrypha, perhaps because

3. See George Newton Conklin, *Biblical Criticism and Heresy in Milton* (New York, 1949), for a discussion of Milton's hermeneutics and exegetical techniques.

4. Madeleine S. Miller and J. Lane Miller, *The New Harper's Bible Dictionary* (New York, 1973), p. 25.

5. William Riley Parker, *Milton: A Biography* (Oxford, 1968), II, 1122.

6. The Book of Enoch, from which Milton indirectly derived some important details, influenced New Testament thought more than any other work in the Pseudepigrapha, according to R. H. Charles, *The Apocrypha and Pseudepigrapha of the Old Testament* (Oxford, 1913), II, 180–81. Although it was apparently inaccessible in the seventeenth century, some of its contents were available through intermediaries. In Jude 6 and 14 there are allusions to Enoch, and the Geneva translators' notes state that "this saying of Enoch" may have been "written in some of those bookes which now remaine not."

the books which Protestants like Milton would refer to as apocryphal would be considered canonical by Roman Catholics, a difference in usage which has caused much confusion and helped to obscure the unique contributions of the apocryphal books. Thus in *Milton and Christian Heroism,* Burton O. Kurth asserts that Renaissance biblical narrative poems explored "three main Scriptural subject matters: the hexameral, the Old Testament, and the New Testament";[7] yet he deals with apocryphal sources in his text without making any differentiation from the Old Testament.

Among those who do refer specifically to the Apocrypha, James Holly Hanford and James G. Taaffe set the tone in *A Milton Handbook:*

> Beyond the canonical books of the Bible there was also the Apocrypha, which would have enjoyed in Milton's mind an only slightly diminished prestige. The Book of Enoch contained a statement as to the fall of the angels, and Milton derived from it at least the name of Satan's standard-bearer, Azazael. His employment of Raphael as the genial messenger of God to Adam in his innocence was suggested by the Book of Tobit, where this angel is the helpful guide and companion of the hero through his several adventures.[8]

But it is misleading to speak of the Apocrypha as enjoying "an only slightly diminished prestige," for although Milton regarded the apocryphal authors as "closest to the scriptures in authority,"[9] the difference between canonical and noncanonical was for him a vitally important one. To Milton, the greatest possible distinction among writings was the distinction between divine and human.

Further, for Protestants like Milton, the Book of Enoch is not one of the fourteen books of the Old Testament Apocrypha; rather, it is one of the books termed the Pseudepigrapha. Even if

7. Berkeley, 1959; reprint ed., Hamden, Conn., 1966, p. 5.

8. Fifth ed. (New York, 1970), p. 203.

9. *Complete Prose Works of John Milton* (CPW), ed. Don M. Wolfe et al. (New Haven, 1953–), VI, 306. Milton's assessment of the Apocrypha's subordination appears in *Christian Doctrine* (CPW, VI, 574–75); but in practice he sometimes handled the Apocrypha more favorably than his theories indicate: cf. CPW, III, 258; VI, 306, 578; and the examples discussed in the text above. He used references to the Apocrypha's lack of doctrinal authority sardonically in CPW, III, 321–22 and III, 538; see also *The Works of John Milton,* ed. Frank Allen Patterson et al. (New York, 1931–38), IX, 121–23.

the book had been accessible in the seventeenth century, as a Protestant Milton would not have considered it equal in authority with the Apocrypha proper. In fact, while it is true that Milton may have derived the name Azazel from Enoch as quoted in the *Chronographia* of Georgius Syncellus (published in 1657) or from the cabalistic tradition via Fludd, Reuchlin, or others,[10] it is highly significant that the name receives canonical sanction in Leviticus 16:8–26, where one goat is for the Lord and one for Azazel, the evil spirit in the wilderness of Judea ritually connected with the scapegoat released to bear away the sins of the people. (The Geneva note for Leviticus 16:9 asserts simply that in Hebrew the scapegoat "is called Azazel.") Milton was no doubt aware that in Hebrew the word *azazel* is used both as the name of a demon and as the name of a place somewhat akin to Hell,[11] but the reason he chose only the name Azazel out of the *four* standard-bearers of Satan named by Fludd (Samael, Azazel, Azael, and Mahazael) is that of the four, only Azazel is mentioned in the Canon. True to his own assertions, Milton did not neglect canonical support when he could find it.

Thus, because Milton is so precise in his terminology and so insistent on a great gulf between the Word of God and the words of men, the student of his sources should try to be equally precise. Although Milton is fairly pragmatic in his use of evidence, utilizing whatever he needs and praising those authors who happen to provide support for his beliefs, his hierarchy of value among Hebrew materials seems to be as follows: first, the Canon; second, the Apocrypha; third, the Pseudepigrapha and the older midrashim (on an equal basis); finally, the later Jewish legends and commentaries, such as the cabalistic *Zohar* or the *Pseudo-Josephus*.[12]

When the Apocrypha is discussed in conjunction with the Canon, as it is by Harris F. Fletcher in *The Use of the Bible in Milton's Prose* or by James H. Sims in *The Bible in Milton's Epics*,[13] it is justly overshadowed by the importance of the

10. Robert H. West, *Milton and the Angels* (Athens, Ga., 1955), p. 155.

11. Walter M. Abbott et al., *The Bible Reader* (New York, 1969), p. 118.

12. Edward Chauncey Baldwin, "Some Extra-Biblical Semitic Influences upon Milton's Story of the Fall of Man," *Journal of English and Germanic Philology* 28 (1929), 396–97.

13. Harris F. Fletcher, *The Use of the Bible in Milton's Prose*, University of Illinois Studies in Language and Literature, vol. 14, no. 3 (1929); James H. Sims, *The Bible in*

canonical influence. But more attention should be paid to the tone of the Apocrypha as a union of Greek and Hebrew thought,[14] a union which is strikingly present in the mind of Milton. E. M. W. Tillyard remarked that the Elizabethan world picture was a simplified version of the more complicated medieval world picture, which in turn was derived "from an amalgam of Plato and the Old Testament, invented by the Jews of Alexandria and vivified by the new religion of Christ."[15] Since much of the Apocrypha originated among the Alexandrian Jews, it is surprising that the apocryphal books have received so little direct attention in studies of medieval and Renaissance thought, and that they have received only peripheral attention as an ingredient in Milton's thought and art.

Perhaps the briefest way to isolate apocryphal concepts in Milton, as opposed to canonical ones, is to examine the four-page attack on the Apocrypha which appeared in the 1640 edition of the Geneva Version of the Bible, printed in Amsterdam by Thomas Stafford. The attack represents the severe view of the Apocrypha taken by those Calvinists who assembled at the Synod of Dort (1618–19), a synod to which the Church of England sent delegates. In *Christian Doctrine,* Milton wrote that the books called Apocrypha "have nothing like the same authority as the canonical, and are not admitted as evidence in deciding points of faith"—and gave four fairly commonplace reasons, three of which appear also in the Geneva Version's "Admonition . . . Concerning the Apocrypha-Books": that they are never cited in the New Testament (by which he apparently means that they are never cited by name by any New Testament author), that they contain much which contradicts the Canon, and that they contain some things which are "fantastic, low, trifling, and quite foreign to real sagacity and religion" (see n. 8). The fourth reason the Genevans gave for rejecting the Apocrypha was the somewhat inaccurate charge that these books were not considered canonical by the Primitive Church. By contrast, Milton's fourth reason was that the apocryphal books were not written in Hebrew and therefore could not have been written for

---

Milton's Epics (Gainesville, Fla., 1962).

14. See Moses Hadas, *The Apocrypha,* tr. Edgar J. Goodspeed (New York, 1938; reprint ed., 1959), p. xvi.

15. *The Elizabethan World Picture* (1943; reprint ed., New York, n.d.), p. 4.

Jews. Apparently he was unaware of the linguistic practices of the Jews in Alexandria.

To substantiate its charge that the Apocrypha contradicts the Canon, the Geneva "Admonition" lists among others the following points of difference: apocryphal teaching of mortalism, freedom of the will, divorce for reasons other than adultery, lying when justified by expediency, and the creation of the Wisdom of God, which "gainsayeth and makes of no force the cleare testimony of the Prophet *Salomon* about the Eternity of the Son of God, Prov. 8:22." No student of Milton needs to be told that these apocryphal doctrines form part of Milton's thinking. Admittedly, Milton's apocryphal views do not necessarily argue a direct influence, for it is probable that Milton's understanding of the Canon led him to conclusions which were sometimes contrary to current views of canonical meaning and similar to those of apocryphal authors.

On the other hand, Milton's familiarity with the Apocrypha cannot be measured by the number of times he cites apocryphal passages as proof-texts, for to do so was contrary to his own principle that the Apocrypha could not be used as proof of a doctrine's validity. Milton did, however, cite the Apocrypha occasionally in reinforcement of a doctrine he felt he had already proven from canonical authority. Examples are his several uses of Ecclesiasticus in *Doctrine and Discipline of Divorce* and *Tetrachordon* to reinforce the validity of divorce for incompatibility.[16] And a major example is the use of texts from Wisdom 11:17 and II Maccabees 7:28 to back up Hebrews 11:3 as proof that God utilized preexistent matter in the Creation, as opposed to creating out of nothing.[17]

In poetry, where he was not arguing but rather creating imaginative experience for his readers, Milton borrowed details freely from apocryphal books, especially details concerning angels and demons. Only two of Milton's four chief angels, Michael and Gabriel, are named *as angels* in the Canon; the

16. See *CPW*, II, 271–72 and 617. The texts Milton cites are Ecclus. 13:16, 37:27, and 25:26.

17. *CPW*, VI, 306. In "Milton's Use of Biblical Quotations," *Journal of English and Germanic Philology* 26 (1927), 154, Harris F. Fletcher points out that the Vulgate version of both verses clearly indicates creation *ex nihilo;* but Milton follows the Junius version, which indicates creation from preexistent materials.

other two, Uriel and Raphael, come from II Esdras and Tobit respectively.[18] In each case, Milton has retained the character of the angel as presented in the Apocrypha; Uriel, who communicated with Esdras in a very lordly fashion, plays a similarly lordly role in *Paradise Lost,* while Raphael, who travels and converses familiarly with Tobias in the Book of Tobit, is Milton's "affable Archangel."[19]

Milton alludes to the Book of Tobit several times in *Paradise Lost,* stressing the role of "sociable" Raphael as the securer of marital happiness and of Asmodeus as a destroyer thereof.[20] The equation of Asmodeus with fleshly lust and Raphael with sociable geniality illuminates Milton's concept of true conjugal love, "Founded in Reason," as a great creative force, and of "adulterous lust" as a destructive characteristic worthy only of "bestial herds" (*PL* IV.750–62). In *Paradise Regained* (II.151–52), Milton describes Belial as the most dissolute and sensual of all the fallen angels, "and after *Asmodai* / The fleshliest Incubus." This characterization of Asmodeus, in keeping with his role of the demon-lover of Sara and the murderer of her seven pagan husbands, completes the symbolism which Milton derives from the apocryphal narrative. Raphael the healer, the obedient messenger of God, is pitted against Asmodeus, the destoyer and the lustful, so that Raphael's personal triumph over Asmodeus in the Heavenly War symbolizes the ultimate triumph of right reason over passion, and of the forces of creation over those of destruction.[21] But on the earth, whereas obedience to Raphael's instructions to Tobias resulted in the immediate defeat of Asmodeus and the ideal marriage with Sara, disobedience to Raphael's instructions to Adam resulted in the marring of the ideal marriage and thus in the temporary victory of Asmodeus-like Satan. Milton introduces Satan into the Garden of Eden by comparing his pleasure at the Garden's sweet smell with Asmodeus's horror and defeat because of the smelly fumes from

18. Raphael and Uriel are also mentioned frequently in the psuedepigraphal books, especially in the Book of Enoch; and the name Uriel is used for human beings in I and II Chronicles.

19. *PL* VII.41. But Milton borrows from Tobit 12:15 a description of Raphael for his introduction of Uriel in *PL* III.648–51.

20. *PL* IV.166–71; V.219–23; VI.362–68.

21. *PL* VI.362–68.

the fish heart and liver burnt in the bedroom at Raphael's suggestion. Thus by an apocryphal allusion Milton foreshadows Satan's ultimate defeat just at the threshold of his temporary victory.[22]

Some of the details of Hell in Book I of *Paradise Lost* probably reflect the powerful account of the Egyptian plague of darkness in Wisdom 17:

> For when unrighteous men thought to oppress the holy nation; they being shut up in their houses, the prisoners of darkness, and fettered with the bonds of a long night, lay [there] exiled from the eternal providence. . . . No power of the fire might give them light. . . . Only there appeared unto them a fire kindled of itself, very dreadful. . . . So then whosoever there fell down was straitly kept, shut up in a prison without iron bars. . . . for they were all bound with one chain of darkness. . . . Over them only was spread an heavy night, an image of that darkness which should afterward receive them: but yet were they unto themselves more grievous than the darkness.[23]

The whole atmosphere of Milton's Hell, with its strong suggestion of psychological horror that surpasses physical horror, as well as his description of Hell's flames as darkness visible, fed with "ever-burning Sulphur unconsum'd" (69), and a "Prison ordain'd / In utter darkness" (71–72) seems to draw upon this passage. So perhaps does the Chorus's description of Samson as dwelling in "Prison within Prison / Inseparably dark" (*SA* 153–54).

The Dantesque metamorphoses of the fallen angels into serpents and of Satan into "A monstrous Serpent . . . punisht in the shape he sinn'd" (X.514 ff.) parallel the Wisdom of Solomon as well as certain classical and medieval sources, for Wisdom 11:16 promises that "wherewithal a man sinneth, by the same shall he be punished." The context in Wisdom refers to the Egyptians, who were punished by "a multitude of unreasonable beasts" because "being deceived they worshipped serpents void of reason" (11:15). Satan's humiliation, like that of the Egyptians,

---

22. *PL* IV.166–71. Cf. Arnold Stein's discussion of this allusion in *Answerable Style: Essays on* Paradise Lost (Minneapolis, 1953; reprint ed., 1967), p. 59.

23. Apocryphal quotations are from the Authorized Version (Oxford, n.d.). Milton used the Authorized Version in English and in Latin the Junius-Tremellius (Protestant) version.

perfectly fits his crime; he had incarnated himself in a serpent for the irrational act of destroying God's creation, and had pretended to Eve that the fruit of the Tree of Knowledge had made the serpent more reasonable. Now, at the moment of his triumph, he is changed into an irrational serpent without the power of speech and without even the ability to stop biting into the delicious-looking fruit which repeatedly turns to ashes in his mouth (X.560–72).[24]

In *Paradise Regained* (III.163–70), Milton causes Satan to reveal his own character by means of an extensive allusion to the apocryphal books of the Maccabees. Satan asks Christ,

> think'st thou to regain
> Thy right by sitting still or thus retiring?
> So did not *Maccabaeus:* he indeed
> Retir'd unto the Desert, but with arms;
> And o'er a mighty King so oft prevail'd,
> That by strong hand his Family obtain'd,
> Though Priests, the Crown, and *David's* Throne usurp'd,
> With *Modin* and her Suburbs once content.

The Satanic slant of this recital becomes obvious if it is compared with the apocryphal account. For example, according to II Maccabees 5:27, "Judas Maccabeus with nine others, or thereabout, withdrew himself into the wilderness, and lived in the mountains after the manner of beasts, with his company, who fed on herbs continually, lest they should be partakers of the pollution." Satan perverts the story from the daring and high-minded attempt of human beings to save themselves and their country from pollution into the successful attempt of a power-hungry family to seize the throne of David. Once *content* with their own small town, Satan says, the Maccabees *obtained* the crown by a strong hand and by priestly aid—using both force and religion for their own ends—thus successfully *usurping* David's throne. Nothing could be more revelatory of Satan's

24. According to the pseudepigraphal Books of Adam and Eve, when Satan asked the serpent for help in getting Adam thrown out of Paradise, the serpent hesitated, fearing the Lord's anger. The devil assured the serpent that together they could deceive the Lord, and the serpent gave consent (Apocalypse Mosis 16:1–5). As punishment the serpent lost his speech as well as his ears, wings, arms, and legs (26:1–4). Another of the Pseudepigrapha, the Book of Jubilees (3:28), explains that all animals lost the gift of speech as a result of Adam's Fall—a belief shared by Josephus, Philo, and many others.

character than this projection of his motivations and methods into the minds of other and purer creatures.[25]

In the prose, where evidence "is all," Milton is more cautious and uses more qualifiers concerning his borrowings from the Apocrypha, his attitude closely resembling that of John Calvin.[26] Like Calvin, Milton feels free to use an apocryphal text to bolster his own argument even while taking issue with certain possible interpretations of the text. His fullest prose use of an apocryphal passage occurs in *Eikonoklastes* and involves a detailed summary and interpretation of I Esdras 3:1–4:63. He begins by equating the authority of Esdras with that of Josephus: "It happn'd once, as we find in *Esdras* and *Josephus,* Authors not less beleiv'd than any under sacred, to be a great and solemn debate in the Court of *Darius,* what thing was to be counted strongest of all other."[27] Like Calvin, Milton here distinguishes

25. For an extensive list of apocryphal allusions and parallels in Milton's poetry and prose, see Virginia R. Mollenkott, "Milton and the Apocrypha" (Ph.D. diss., New York University, 1964). It is obviously beyond the scope of the present paper to deal at length with the influence of the Pseudepigrapha on Milton, but Eric Smith suggests a promising field of inquiry in his assertion that "whenever the Fall of the Angels gained wide acceptance as a myth, it is not recorded in any developed form in canonical writings, but only in apocryphal books from about the second century B.C. and in later Rabbinical and Patristic commentaries" (*Some Versions of the Fall* [Pittsburgh, 1973], p. 211). Strictly speaking, however, the chief extracanonical sources concerning the fall of the angels are not apocryphal but pseudepigraphal: particularly I and II Enoch and the Vita Adae et Evae. Especially interesting for Miltonists is the fact that in the Vita, the unfallen Satan was asked to worship the image of God in newly created man, and refused on the basis of seniority, for which refusal he and his angels were expelled from heaven. Since the Son is known in the New Testament as God's perfect image and as the Second Adam, and in *PL* jealousy over the Son's "begetting" was the cause of Satan's rebellion, the parallels are well-nigh irresistible.

26. Calvin's attitude toward the Apocrypha is clearly evidenced by a passage in the *Institutes* concerning the interpretation of Ecclus. 15:14. Commenting that the supporters of free will make use of this passage, although it is from a book "which is well known to be . . . of doubtful authority," Calvin proceeds, "Let it be granted, that man at his creation was endowed with a power of choosing life or death. What if we reply, that he has lost it? . . . Therefore I reply . . . to Ecclesiasticus himself, whoever he be: If you design to teach man to seek within himself a power to attain salvation, your authority is not so great in our estimation as to obtain even the smallest degree of credit, in opposition to the undoubted word of God. But if you only aim to repress the malignity of the flesh, which vainly attempts to vindicate itself by transferring its crimes to God, and you therefore reply, that man was originally endued with rectitude, from which it is evident that he was the cause of his own ruin, I readily assent to it" (*Institutes of the Christian Religion,* tr. John Allen [Philadelphia, 1932], I, 303–4).

27. *CPW,* III, 582–83.

two kinds of literature, the sacred or divinely inspired and the human; the implication is that once a work has taken its place among human writings, it must earn its position by means of its own reasonableness and power.

Milton then goes on to recount the story of the three noble guardsmen who tried to prove what power on earth was strongest, and of how Zorobabel won the prize by proving that "neither Wine, nor Women, nor the King, but Truth, of all other things was the strongest." But Milton asserts that he must either reinterpret the apocryphal meaning, by assuming that truth and justice are identical, or must differ from Esdras, by insisting that active justice "by her office" in the affairs of mankind is stronger than truth can be. Milton even goes so far as to paraphrase I Esdras 4:40, inserting his own word, *Justice,* where the apocryphal author had used *Truth*—a liberty Milton would not have taken with the canonical Scriptures: "We may conclude therfor that Justice, above all other things, is and ought to be the strongest; Shee is the strength, the Kingdom, the power, and majestie of all Ages." And he insists, "Truth her self would subscribe to this, though *Darius* and all the Monarchs of the World should deny"—thus twisting the Apocrypha's statement of the primacy of truth into support for his own concept of the primacy of justice. This assertion brings Milton to his major point: he wants to do a work not much inferior to that of Zorobabel, by placing the English people under justice rather than under kings. "But if a King may doe among men whatsoever is his will and pleasure, and notwithstanding be unaccountable to men, then contrary to this magnifi'd wisdom of *Zorobabel,* neither Truth nor Justice, but the King is strongest of all other things: which that Persian Monarch himself in the midst of all his pride and glory durst not assume."[28] By demonstrating that righteous accountability of king to subject is older and has greater historical and rational sanction than the theory of Divine Right of Kings, Milton has molded the apocryphal story into a powerful political weapon. The fact that Irene Samuel discusses this very passage as an instance of Milton's use of Platonic Ideas[29] only serves to stress the Greek and often specifically

28. *CPW*, III, 583–85.
29. *Plato and Milton* (Ithaca, 1947; reprint ed., 1965), p. 141.

Platonic tone of much of the Apocrypha. And the fact that she omits mention of the Apocrypha's role indicates the need in Milton scholarship of greater awareness of the apocryphal influence as the source nearest in authority to that of the canonical Scriptures.

Though immeasurable, the influence of the Apocrypha on the Renaissance concept of right reason must have been extensive. In the case of Milton, who was perhaps its most powerful exponent, it is probable that some of the rationalism and Platonism in *Comus* and *Paradise Lost* came to him by way of the Apocrypha. At the very least, the identification of knowledge with virtue in the Wisdom literature would have caused him to be more trustful of Hellenism.

The Apocrypha's emphasis on the worthy life as the life of virtue based upon reason, including of course the knowledge of God, is more insistent than that of the Old Testament Canon and differs widely from the apparent suspicion of intellect in the New Testament. Consider, for instance, Wisdom 9:17—10:3:

And thy counsel who hath known, except thou give wisdom, and send thy Holy Spirit from above? For so the ways of them which lived on the earth were reformed, and men were taught the things that are pleasing unto thee, and were saved through wisdom. She preserved the first formed father of the world, that was created alone, and brought him out of his fall, And gave him power to rule all things. But when the unrighteous went away from her in his anger, he perished also in the fury wherewith he murdered his brother.

This passage is full of the emphases of Renaissance Christian humanism: that wisdom is God's gift; that it can reform and save mankind; that it brought Adam "out of his fall" so that he might regain the dominion which the human race had originally been assigned; and that passion is a desertion of reason, a desertion which leads to self-destruction. As Milton put it, "The end then of learning is to repair the ruins of our first parents by regaining to know God aright, and out of that knowledge to love him, to imitate him, and to be like him, as we may the neerest by possessing our souls of true virtue, which being united to the heavenly grace of faith, makes up the highest perfection."[30]

30. "Of Education," *CPW*, II, 366–67.

To some readers Milton sounds suspiciously rationalistic, as if mankind could achieve self-salvation by means of reasonable behavior; thus the *Milton Handbook* proclaims that Milton "seems to have felt instinctively that man's salvation depends upon himself."[31] But Milton, like other Renaissance Christian humanists, no doubt felt comfortable with rationalistic-sounding phrases because of the example of apocryphal usage. Perry Miller ventures an explanation for the rise of rationalism which implicates the Apocrypha: "Man in the seventeenth century did not see the dangers ahead, the possibility that such descriptions of faith in the terms of right reason . . . could give rise to a naturalistic morality and a belief that education would achieve everything usually ascribed to grace, because they were convinced that theology would remain forever the norm of reason."[32] Small wonder that men in the seventeenth century did not see the danger of describing faith in terms of right reason, when bound between the covers of the Authorized Version of the Bible they had ample apocryphal precedent for doing so! Not only was there the statement that men were "saved through wisdom" (Wisd. 9:18); there were also passages which promised that "to be allied unto wisdom is immortality" (Wisd. 8:17); and there was the entire emphasis of the Book of Ecclesiasticus. As W. O. E. Oesterley points out,

the identification of virtue with knowledge is a distinct Hellenic trait, and is treated in . . . [Ecclesiasticus] as axiomatic; in the past, human and divine wisdom had been regarded as opposed, whereas owing to Greek influence, in Ecclesiasticus, as well as in the Wisdom literature generally, it is taught that Wisdom is the one thing of all others which is indispensable to him who would lead a godly life.[33]

While it is true that the Book of Proverbs also personifies and extols Wisdom, the emphasis in Proverbs and other Old Testament books is on just behavior and obedience to God's laws rather than on knowledge as such, and the terminology and tone is less rationalistic than that of the apocryphal books.

Milton is more careful than many Renaissance Christian

31. Hanford and Taaffe, *Milton Handbook*, p. 115.
32. *The New England Mind: The Seventeenth Century* (New York, 1939), p. 202.
33. *An Introduction to the Books of the Apocrypha* (1935; reprint ed., London, 1946), p. 11.

humanists to distinguish between Hellenism and Hebraism, knowledge and wisdom/virtue, reason and faith; but like the Apocrypha, he insists on' the necessity of integrating them if a person is to be truly wise. Beyond all renewal lies the power of God; for wisdom is the gift of God and right reason is fully possible only in the regenerate, as witness Wisdom 9:17 ("send thy Holy Spirit from above") and *Paradise Lost* III.169–80:

> Son of my bosom, Son who art alone
> My world, my wisdom, and effectual might,
>
> .   .   .   .
>
> Man shall not quite be lost, but sav'd who will,
> Yet not of will in him, but grace in me
> Freely voutsaf't; once more I will renew
> His lapsed powers, though forfeit and enthrall'd
> By sin to foul exorbitant desires;
> Upheld by me, yet once more he shall stand
> On even ground against his mortal foe,
> By me upheld . . .[34]

The Apocrypha also influenced Milton's picture of what would have happened had Adam and Eve never fallen. Since the Canon makes no direct statements concerning this point, it has been assumed that Milton turned to Plato; but it is more probable, because of his hierarchy of values, that he derived the concept of unfallen mankind's immortality from Wisdom 1:13–15:

For God made not death: neither hath he pleasure in the destruction of the living. For he created all things, that they might have their being: and the generations of the world were healthful; and there is no poison of destruction in them, nor the kingdom of death upon the earth: (For righteousness is immortal).

Wisdom 2:23–24 is even more explicit:

For God created man to be immortal, and made him to be an image of his own eternity. Nevertheless through envy of the devil came death into the world: and they that do hold of his side do find it.

Raphael explains to Adam that in the unfallen creation, body will work its way up to spirit; and Adam in turn praises Raphael for describing how "By steps we may ascend to God" (V.478–512). In

---

34. All quotations from Milton's poetry are from John Milton, *Complete Poems and Major Prose*, ed. Merritt Y. Hughes (New York, 1957).

this connection Irene Samuel remarks that those critics are in error who presume that the Fall was a necessary prelude to the highest happiness; such critics assume that good could never have been known except through the knowledge of evil.[35] It was in order to warn against this idea that Milton introduced his passages about the gradual growth and felicitous' immortality of unfallen humanity.[36] Adam and Eve were created, and would increasingly have become within their respective limitations the images of God's own eternity if they had been "found obedient," and had retained "Unalterably firm his love entire." But, of course, as the Apocrypha puts it, envious Satan brought death into the world. The apocryphal Wisdom of Solomon is thus one of the sources of the Platonism inherent in Milton's concept of unfallen humanity and hence in his repudiating the doctrine of the Fortunate Fall.

For the peculiar combination of Hebraic morality and Platonic expression which characterizes *Comus,* one must look primarily to the Apocrypha rather than to the canonical Scriptures. The Attendant Spirit bears similarities to the many-faceted but essentially single muse of Milton's invocations, and to the Hebraic concept of Wisdom as developed in Proverbs and especially in the Wisdom of Solomon. In the opening lines of the masque, the Attendant Spirit announces that he has descended from the very presence of God on an errand only to those who "by due steps aspire / To lay their just hands on that Golden Key / That opes the Palace of Eternity." Similarly, according to the Apocrypha, Wisdom descends from the very presence of God (Wisd. 9:4, 9–10) and enters only into "holy souls" (Wisd. 7:27). Therefore, to follow the Attendant Spirit is to follow Wisdom, and this may be done only by loving virtue. Injunctions to achieve wisdom through virtuous obedience occur everywhere in the Apocrypha; for instance, "If thou desire wisdom, keep the commandments, and the Lord shall give her unto thee" (Ecclus. 1:26). Such wisdom renders a person fearless, for "fear is nothing else but a betraying of the succours which reason offereth" (Wisd. 17:12). A similar equation of right behavior with wisdom and knowledge occurs in the Old and New Testaments, of course, but there it is for the most part stripped of any Hellenistic aura and oriented more exclusively toward lawful

35. *Plato and Milton,* p. 116.

36. See Virginia R. Mollenkott, "Milton's Rejection of the Fortunate Fall," *Milton Quarterly* 6 (1972), 1–5.

behavior and correct doctrine rather than reasonableness, as when Christ promises, "If any man will do his will, he shall know of the doctrine" (John 7:17). As for the "due steps" to which the righteous aspire in order to climb toward Eternity's palace, they are outlined in Wisdom 6:17–20: "For the very true beginning of her [Wisdom] is the desire of discipline; and the care of discipline is love; And love is the keeping of her laws; and the giving heed unto her laws is the assurance of incorruption; And incorruption maketh us near unto God: Therefore the desire of wisdom bringeth to a kingdom."

Milton carefully restricted the use of a Platonic continuum of steps rising gradually toward God to just two areas: prelapsarian humanity and regenerate humanity.[37] Never did he apply the concept to fallen and unredeemed mankind, for such an application would have implied that by its own efforts mankind could achieve salvation. These restrictions are of course governed by Milton's whole theological system, but they drew some of their details from apocryphal sources. For instance, *Paradise Lost* (III.515–30) describes Jacob's vision of stairs in terms reminiscent both of the Platonic ladder and of the steps outlined in the passage quoted above from the Wisdom of Solomon, in which the Platonic influence is almost universally recognized. Each Stair mysteriously was meant," Milton tells us, and furthermore, the stairs opened onto "A passage down to th' Earth, a passage wide, / Wider by far than that of after-times." This concept of free access to God in the prelapsarian world and difficulty of access in the postlapsarian world is implied in the Canon, but is stated outright in the Apocrypha:

when Adam transgressed my statutes, then was decreed that now is done. Then were the entrances of this world made narrow, full of sorrow and travail: they are but few and evil, full of perils, and very painful. For the entrances of the elder world were wide and sure, and brought immortal fruit. (II Esdras 7:11–13).

The Apocrypha's details, including the immortal fruit (*PL* XI.285) obviously appealed to Milton's imagination.

37. Like Milton, Calvin interpreted Plato's ladder of perfection as applying either to unfallen or fallen-and-redeemed mankind. See *Institutes,* I, 53.

On the other hand, *Comus* applies the Platonic/apocryphal imagery of "due steps" to human beings who have "just hands"— that is, only to the children of the Lord, the justified, the regenerate. The opening lines of *Comus* draw a contrast between those who are "Unmindful of the crown that Virtue gives / After this mortal change" and those who aspire to climb the steps to the Palace of Eternity. Just as the speaker of these words, the Attendant Spirit, is characterized in terms of the personification of Wisdom in the apocryphal book by that name, so the very wording of the contrast echoes the Apocrypha. II Esdras 2:45 speaks of "they that have put off the mortal clothing, and put on the immortal . . . now are they crowned, and receive palms." It is true that the Canon also implies the metaphor of changing from mortality to immortality as if one were changing clothes (I Corinthians 15:53), but II Esdras makes the metaphor explicit. And while the canonical passage moves on to a paean of triumph over death, the apocryphal one specifies, like Milton, that after the "mortal change" comes "the crown." Thus in this case the apocryphal source is more probable than the canonical one; and at the same time the verbal echoes provide reassurance that Milton's characteristic blend of Hebraism and Hellenism is to some degree directly traceable to the Apocrypha.

The Apocrypha establishes godliness as a prerequisite to right reason in passages which are more powerfully developed than any in the canonical Scriptures, and here again the strength of the apocryphal linkage is echoed in Milton. For instance, Wisdom 1:4–5 asserts that "into a malicious soul wisdom shall not enter; nor dwell in the body that is subject unto sin. For the holy spirit of discipline will flee deceit, and remove from thoughts that are without understanding, and will not abide when unrighteousness cometh in." Similarly in *Christian Doctrine* Milton connects wisdom with godliness (to him possible, as we have seen, only in the regenerate): "Wisdom is the virtue by which we earnestly search out God's will, cling to it with all diligence once we have understood it, and govern all our actions by its rule."[38] What

---

38. *CPW*, VI, 647. The fact that Milton cites Prov. 23:9 instead of one of the more powerful apocryphal passages indicates his principle concerning canonical support for doctrine, rather than any lack of awareness of the apocryphal sanction.

Robert Hoopes wrote about the Cambridge Platonists applies just as precisely to Milton and to the apocryphal authors of Wisdom and Ecclesiasticus: "When . . . [they] exalt the faculty of reason, they are not glorifying unrestrained intellection, but the power of mind wholly dedicated to the service of . . . faith."[39]

Milton's treatment of the *de casibus virorum* theme in *Samson Agonistes* (164–75) differs significantly from traditional treatments of the theme, and the key to the difference lies in the Apocrypha: "Wisdom lifteth up the head of him that is of low degree, and maketh him to sit among great men. . . . exalt not thyself in the day of honour: for the works of the Lord are wonderful, and his works among men are hidden. Many kings have sat down upon the ground; and one that was never thought of hath worn the crown. Many mighty men have been mightily disgraced; and the honourable delivered into other men's hands" (Ecclus. 11:1–6). Canonical passages also deal with the *de casibus* theme, but compared to Ecclesiasticus they appear somewhat abstract, as in the famous "Pride goeth before destruction, and a haughty spirit before a fall" (Prov. 16:18; cf. Prov. 11:2, 12:7, 18:2, 29:23). One suspects that many medieval and Renaissance treatments of the *de casibus* theme were influenced by the Ecclesiasticus passage,[40] for a careless reading of it leads to the assumption that it supports the medieval concept of the fall of great men as simply a matter of fate or fortune's caprice, while a closer look reveals that in the Apocrypha as in Milton the change of degree, while not entirely under human control, is largely a matter of wisdom in the individual.

Because the passage is easy to misinterpret, it is worth quoting what Milton has to say about the fall of the formerly great. The Chorus begins by making Samson's predicament a mirror of the condition of fallen mankind:

39. *Right Reason in the English Renaissance* (Cambridge, Mass., 1962), p. 177.

40. Cf. Shakespeare, *Richard II,* act 3, sc. 3, ll. 155–56; "For God's sake, let us sit upon the ground / And tell sad stories of the death of kings." In *Shakespeare's Biblical Knowledge . . . as Exemplified in the Plays of the First Folio* (London, 1935), pp. 290–92, Richmond Noble lists some of Shakespeare's apocryphal allusions as follows: two to I Esdras; one to II Esdras; four to Tobit; three to Judith; fourteen to Wisdom; no fewer than fifty-eight to Ecclesiasticus; two to Baruch; two to Susanna; one to Bel and the Dragon; two to I Maccabees; and one to II Maccabees. Noble's list is not all-inclusive.

O mirror of our fickle state,
Since man on earth unparallel'd!
The rarer thy example stands,
By how much from the top of wondrous glory,
Strongest of mortal men,
To lowest pitch of abject fortune thou art fall'n.
For him I reckon not in high estate
Whom long descent of birth
Or the sphere of fortune raises;
But thee whose strength, while virtue was her mate,
Might have subdu'd the Earth,
Universally crown'd with highest praises.

This passage is not "an example of decline through chance,"[41] for the Chorus takes pains to refute the doctrine of chance: a man is not great because of his birth or because he has been raised by the "sphere of fortune"; he is great when he has a combination of strength and virtue. This implies that Samson's fall came about through a loss of virtue; and it is this sort of fall, not a decline through chance, which is a "mirror of our fickle state." Accordingly, the Chorus sees Samson's former greatness and present blindness and captivity as a mirror of the instability of the human condition—a rare and unparalleled mirror, because Samson fell from the very highest to the very lowest. Like humanity in the original Fall and like the unwise and disgraced kings in Ecclesiasticus, Samson fell not through chance but through his own loss of virtue/wisdom. Accordingly, Samson bemoans his fate, wondering why his birth was surrounded by supernatural favors when through his own failure his life has turned out to be so grim. His attitude and his being held up as a "mirror of man's fickle state" bring to mind another apocryphal passage: "For what profit is it unto us, if there be promised us an immortal time, whereas we have done the works that bring death?" (II Esdras 7:49).

Concerning the Platonic doctrine of Ideas, the Apocrypha clarified an obscure canonical passage to provide the scriptural sanction so important to Milton. Milton's suggestion that perhaps things on earth are shadows of heavenly archetypes should not be

---

41. So John Shawcross labelled it in the first edition (New York, 1963) of *The Complete English Poetry of John Milton*, p. 156, n. 25. However he corrected the error in the second edition (Garden City, N.Y., 1971), p. 580, n. 27.

traced exclusively to Greek thought, for the concept appears to have been fairly common in Semitic literature. It is hinted at in Exodus 25:9: "According to all that I show thee, after the pattern of the tabernacle, and the pattern of all the instruments thereof, even so shall ye make it." This passage is alluded to in Hebrews 8:5 as illustration that priests serve "unto the example and shadow of heavenly things." But the concept of a heavenly archetype was very clearly stated almost two hundred years earlier in the Apocrypha: "Thou hast commanded me to build a temple upon thy holy mount . . . a resemblance [copy] of the holy tabernacle, which thou hast prepared from the beginning" (Wisd. 9:8). Irene Samuel proved that Milton was interested in the Platonic doctrine of the Idea, which he interpreted as "a pattern in the creative mind, divine or human, according to which a world or a treatise or a series of events may be shaped."[42] It may be even more significant to recognize the complementary role of the Canon and the Apocrypha in shaping Raphael's hint that earth may be "the shadow of Heav'n" and that he is therefore going to liken "spiritual to corporal forms" (*PL* V.571–76). Awareness of such scriptural sources is especially important when one is dealing with a poet who overtly made it a practice to subordinate all classical learning to "the determinat sentence of *David*, or *Salomon*, or the Evangels and *Apostolic* scriptures."[43]

To conclude: the rationalistic tone of the Apocrypha, combining a Hellenic questioning with a Hebraic sense of duty to God, is a pervasive influence on the whole tradition of Christian humanism. Not only did Milton respond to this general atmosphere, especially in his concept of right reason, but many of his other concepts show an interesting apocryphal bent: in the doctrine of sex and chastity, where Milton's views often parallel those of Jesus the Son of Sirach, author of Ecclesiasticus; in the expression of omnipresence verging upon pantheism; and in the doctrines of creation from preexistent matter, of earth as the mother of all mankind, of free will, of expedient lying, of for-

42. *Plato and Milton*, p. 134. Recent commentators see the Platonic doctrine of the world as image or copy in Hebrews 10:1; but sixteenth- and seventeenth-century commentators took "shadow" to mean merely "shadow cast by a body" or "silhouette or outline." See William G. Madsen, *From Shadowy Types to Truth* (New Haven, 1968), pp. 96–98.

43. "Of Education," *CPW*, II, 397.

bidden knowledge, and of mortalism. But claims for direct apocryphal influence on Milton's doctrines must be muted because of Milton's obvious subordination of every concept to his interpretation of canonical meaning. As George Newton Conklin claims, "With Milton's hermeneutics definitely propounded and his exegetical equipment and technique so manifest, there may be no great need to search for the sources of his theological irregularities. It is quite probable that the ideas, the reasoning, and the proofs are wholly Milton's; the parallels, wherever they occur, merely coincidental."[44]

Milton's poetic derivations from the Apocrypha include details of angelology as well as certain extracanonical details about Hell. His speculations about what would have happened had mankind remained sinless reflect the Platonism of the Apocrypha perhaps more than the direct influence of Greek philosophy; and the concept of Wisdom in the Apocrypha colored the character of Milton's muse and the muselike Attendant Spirit of *Comus*.[45]

Both in his poetry and in his prose, Milton used the Apocrypha in a fashion which distinctly subordinated it to the Canon. The Apocrypha might be used for historical example, for illustration, or for moral encouragement; and in poetry, the Apocrypha might fill out details where the Canon was sketchy or silent. The same could, of course, be said for pagan authors; for Milton was ready to utilize any vividly concrete material which might lend support or power to his lifelong justification of God's ways to man—so long as that source did not in any way contradict his understanding of the canonical Scriptures.

Milton's imagination was powerfully affected by the Old and New Testaments and the literature surrounding them. Of that surrounding literature, the Old Testament Apocrypha, being the nearest to authoritative in Milton's value system, deserves increased attention from Miltonists.

44. *Biblical Criticism*, p. 5.

45. It is true that Wisdom is personified in Proverbs 9, but her characterization there is more practical, less mystical, than the sublime personification in the apocryphal Wisdom of Solomon. Milton's muse partakes of the apocryphal rather than the canonical aura.

"something like Prophetic strain"

Nature, Poetry, and Milton's Genii

WILLIAM A. ORAM

The central theme of Milton's *Poems* (1645) is poetic conversion—the power of poetry to lead "pagan" man toward
Christian truth. Milton develops this theme in many ways, but it
appears most clearly in his use of genii or guardian spirits such as
the "unseen Genius of the Wood"[1] of *Il Penseroso*. Genii appear in
the *Fifth Elegy*, the *Nativity Ode, Il Penseroso, Arcades, Comus*,
and *Lycidas*, and Milton uses them to articulate a progressive
inquiry into the nature of Nature and a simultaneous examination
of the functions of poetry. Indeed, they are the means by which he
connects these two subjects. In the earlier poems, when Milton is
weighing the value of worldly experience for devout Christians,
the genius is a nature-god whose role develops toward mediation
between Heaven and earth. In the later poems the genius, no
longer simply a nature-god, becomes a poet who also mediates
between Nature and the supernatural. Milton emphasizes the
power of the poet-genius to effect in his listeners a conversion that
purifies what is worldly in them and moves the "pagan" or natural
man—the old Adam—toward the new truth of Christianity. In
Lycidas the drowned swain's resurrection as the "Genius of the
shore" resolves a harsh reexamination of both Nature and poetry.
Thus underlying the disparateness of the major poems in the 1645

1. I. 154. References to Milton's works are based on John Milton, *Complete Poems and
Major Prose*, ed. Merritt Y. Hughes (New York, 1957). In arguing for the unity of the 1645
volume this essay starts from Louis L. Martz's fine essay "The Rising Poet, 1645" in *The
Lyric and Dramatic Milton*, ed. Joseph Summers (New York, 1965), pp. 3–33. Martz
argues persuasively that the book presents a developing portrait of the artist as a young
man. The present essay suggests that the volume also explores the powers of the young
poet's art.

47

volume, and despite their differences of kind and occasion, there is a unifying and developing vision of the transforming power of poetry. These contentions will be developed below.

In classical times the term *genius* already covered several distinct figures, and, by the Renaissance, mythographers such as Conti and Cartari used it to translate the Greek *daimon* and to embrace a variety of deities and their characteristics.[2] The resulting vagueness left much to the imagination of individual poets and permitted them to conflate the characteristics of different genii in a single figure. Yet at the risk of oversimplification, it is convenient to distinguish three kinds of genii. 1) The Roman god of generation. He was sometimes referred to as *gerulus* (a bearer or carrier) and since this was translated into English as "porter" he was often portrayed quite literally as a keeper of gates.[3] 2) Personal genii. Each man was supposed to have two— one good and one bad—who tried to guide his actions. The good genius, often identified with the Christian guardian angel, appeals to man's rational nature and leads his soul toward the light. The bad genius appeals to man's lower nature and leads him to follow fleshly appetites. 3) The spirit of a particular place. Mythogra-

2. The fullest accounts of genii are given in Noel Conti's *Mythologiae, sive Explicationis Fabularum* (1551) and Vicenzio Cartari's *Delle Imagini de gli Dei de gli Antichi* (1556). For much of my treatment of the genius in this section I am indebted to Dewitt T. Starnes, "The Figure Genius in the Renaissance," *Studies in the Renaissance* 11 (1964), 234–44, and C. S. Lewis, "Genius and Genius" in his *Studies in Renaissance Literature,* ed. Walter Hooper (Cambridge, 1966). Lewis distinguishes with great clarity the personal genius and the god of generation; he does not discuss the genius of place. For the genius in antiquity see the article on "Genius" by W. F. Otto in August Friedrich von Pauly and Georg Wissowa, eds., *Real-Encyclopädie der Classichen Altertumswissenschaft* (Stuttgart, 1905), VII, 1155–70. There is a treatment of the development of the genius in the Middle Ages and the Renaissance in three articles by E. C. Knowlton: "The Allegorical Figure Genius," *Classical Philology* 15 (1920), 380–84; "Genius as an Allegorical Figure" *Modern Language Notes* 39 (1924), 89–95; and "The Genii of Spenser," *Studies in Philology* 25 (1928), 439–56. On the genius-figure as it appears in the *Nativity Ode* see Lawrence W. Hyman, "Christ's Nativity and the Pagan Deities," *Milton Studies* 2 (1970), 103–12; on *Comus,* see A. Kent Heiatt, "Milton's Comus and Spenser's False Genius," *University of Toronto Quarterly* 38 (1968–69), 313–18. I am indebted to two important essays by Geoffrey Hartman: "Romantic Poetry and the Genius Loci," in *The Disciplines of Criticism,* ed. Peter Demetz et al., pp. 298–314, and "Toward Literary History," *Daedalus* 99 (1970), 355–83, both reprinted in Hartman, *Beyond Formalism: Literary Essays 1958–70* (New Haven, 1970).

3. Starnes, "Figure Genius" pp. 240–41. The most famous genial porters are Spenser's in his descriptions of the Bower of Bliss (*F.Q.* II.xii.47–49) and the Garden of Adonis (*F.Q.* III.vi.31–32).

phers say little about these figures; they appear in poetry as local and occasionally as national deities.[4]

Milton learned about genii from his classical reading, and he may also have relied on the stock accounts of the figure by Renaissance mythographers and lexicographers. In his early work, however, he is chiefly concerned with the spirit of place, about whom little was written. He uses this figure repeatedly because it raises a problem that is at once poetic and theological. To what degree is the created world itself holy? Can the pagan worship of a single sacred spot be reconciled with the omnipresence of the Christian God? How is the Christian poet justified in evoking such a pagan figure?[5]

These problems are important in the *Nativity Ode,* where the incarnation of Christ begins a new relationship between heaven and earth. And in the *Ode* the treatment of both Nature and the genius is ambivalent. As the speaker describes the angelic symphony he thinks for a moment that it may entirely transform fallen Nature:

> For if such holy Song
> Enwrap our fancy long,
>   Time will run back, and fetch the age of gold,
> And speckl'd vanity
> Will sicken soon and die,
>   And leprous sin will melt from earthly mold,
> And Hell itself will pass away,
> And leave her dolorous mansions to the peering day.

The angelic song transforms its hearers. The marks of the Fall (133–40) in human nature—"speckl'd vanity," "leprous sin"—will simply "melt away." There need not be a catastrophic destruction of the earth or a final division of the sheep and the goats: even

4. National genii occur, as one might expect, in patriotic contexts. There is a Genius of England, Scotland, and Wales in Thomas Carew's *Coelum Brittanicum,* and when Michael Drayton begins his national epic *Poly-Olbion* he invokes the genius of the isle as his muse (First Song, l. 8). It is far more usual, however, for genii to be local spirits. When Robert Herrick calls King Charles a "universal *Genius*" ("To the King Upon his comming with his Army into the West," 1. l. 2) the epithet has the surprise of an oxymoron.

5. The problem is a familiar one in the Renaissance. See the useful discussion in Baxter Hathaway, *Marvels and Commonplaces* (New York, 1968), pp. 133–51. Milton differs in making the literary problem of whether or not to employ pagan figures a specific case of a theological problem: To what degree is the world that God has created itself holy?

Hell will "pass away," allowing all things to be redeemed. But the speaker's extreme optimism is soon qualified. "Wisest Fate" decrees that such a painless transformation cannot take place: redemption involves Christ's death as well as his birth. The harmonizing music of the spheres must yield to the terrifying trump of doom: the world must be destroyed before it can be renewed (149–64).

These alternate versions of Nature's capacity for redemption oppose one another throughout the *Nativity Ode*.[6] Nature feels herself corrupt when Christ is born and covers herself in snow, "Confounded, that her Maker's eyes / Should look so near upon her foul deformities" (43–44). Yet she is also stilled into a magical peace, and the winds rejoice in Christ's coming, "Whispering new joys to the mild Ocean" (66). According to one view, Christ is the supreme mediator, renewing the bond between earth and Heaven; according to the other he is the "dreadful Judge" who will spread his throne in middle air (164). The speaker shifts from one view to the other, never finally opting for either.

This ambivalence in the treatment of Nature extends to the Genius who, with Apollo, begins the list of banished pagan deities. Both gods have been false mediators: they have diverted men's worship from Creator to creature and must be banished when Christ, the true mediator, appears. Yet there is a loss with this gain: the Genius is banished with sorrow.

> The lonely mountains o'er
> And the resounding shore,
>   A voice of weeping heard, and loud lament;
> From haunted spring and dale
> Edg'd with poplar pale,
>   The parting Genius is with sighing sent;
> With flow'r-inwov'n tresses torn
> The Nymphs in twilight shade of tangled thickets mourn.
>
> (181–88)

6. Critics have tended to repeat the opposition which is in the *Ode*. Rosemond Tuve (*Images and Themes in Five Poems by Milton* [Cambridge, Mass., 1957], pp. 37–72) stresses Nature's goodness; J. B. Broadbent ("The Nativity Ode," in *The Living Milton: Essays by Various Hands*, ed. Frank Kermode [London, 1960], pp. 12–31), her corruption. Some recent treatments of the poem have stressed the ambiguity of Milton's treatment (Hyman, "Christ's Nativity") or seen the opposition as part of a historical tension between Christian and pagan religions which Milton dramatizes in the poem (Lawrence W. Kingsley, "Mythic Dialectic in the Nativity Ode," *Milton Studies* 4 [1972], 163–76).

The lines stress a new emptiness in the world. The mountains are "lonely" and the magic enclosures of "spring and dale / Edg'd with poplar pale" will now lack the deities that have haunted them. Milton incorporates in the stanza some of the pathos found in Herbert's "Decay"—the nostalgia for an age in which the holy is accessible in external things. With Christ's coming the twilit deities of Nature vanish and the sacred is closed "in some one corner of a feeble heart" ("Decay," l. 12). Milton uses the conventions of the pastoral elegy (the echoing, sympathetic landscape, the weeping nymphs) to suggest the end of a pagan pastoral existence. As the simple shepherds of the *Ode* look up to the overwhelming music celebrating the "mighty Pan," their old existence is about to be transformed. Future oracles will not be found in Apollo's shrine but in Christ's parables. The twilight of Nature must yield to the dazzling inner light of God's truth.

As Milton develops, his poems increasingly stress the reconciliation of Heaven and earth, avoiding the opposition between them which characterizes much of the *Nativity Ode*. Pagan mythological figures like the genius take on a Christian significance and this syncretism stands as a metaphor for the capacity of divine meaning to infuse and direct one's experience of the world. The reclamation of the guardian spirit begins with the benevolent Genius of *Il Penseroso* but attains its full formulation in *Arcades*. This brief masque presents in almost diagrammatic form the pattern that *Comus* and *Lycidas* will elaborate and refine. As John Wallace suggests, the masque presents the audience with a myth of transition or conversion. The shepherds who have come looking for the Countess-goddess of Derby have lived "By sandy *Ladon's* Lillied banks" (97) in a world of classical pastoral. Their journey involves "a pilgrimage from the profane to the religious, from the classical South to the Christian North" and the Countess at whose throne they worship possesses the radiance of divine sapience.[7] The masquers progress naturally from the pagan to the "mighty" Pan.

The Genius of the Wood who greets the masquers emblemizes this process of conversion. After welcoming the shepherds he describes himself:

7. "Milton's *Arcades*," *Journal of English and Germanic Philology* 58 (1959), 227–36; reprinted in Arthur E. Barker, ed., *Milton: Modern Essays in Criticism* (London, 1965), p. 85.

> For know by lot from *Jove* I am the pow'r
> Of this fair Wood, and live in Oak'n bow'r,
> To nurse the Saplings tall, and curl the grove
> With Ringlets quaint, and wanton windings wove.
> And all my Plants I save from nightly ill,
> Of noisome winds, and blasting vapors chill . . .
>   (44–49)

The Genius now serves a Christianized Jove. He presents to the masquers a world capable of redemption, though it is still subject to the "blasting vapours" and "evil dew" (50) that have come with the fall. His words express a delighted appreciation of his natural charges: the grove is "curled" with "ringlets quaint" and its "wanton windings" suggest a joyous natural art rather than error.[8] The Genius acts as a shepherd, "numbering" his charges (59) and healing them by charms, "puissant words and murmurs made to bless" (60). But the role of shepherd lasts only through twilight. At night when "drowsiness / Hath lockt up mortal sense" (61–62) he shows the capacities of his immortal nature:

> then listen I
> To the celestial *Sirens'* harmony,
> That sit upon the nine infolded Spheres
> And sing to those that hold the vital shears
> And turn the Adamantine spindle round
> On which the fate of gods and men is wound.
>   (62–67)

The Genius is in contact both with the creation at its most humble in plants and trees, and with creating Nature who listens to the celestial Sirens. Milton glosses the music of the spheres in the *Second Prolusion* as "that universal interaction of all things, that lovely concord among them, which Pythagoras poetically symbolized as harmony" and Homer as the golden chain (Hughes, p. 603). The Genius states that this divine harmony "draws" the lower world "in measur'd motion . . . / After the heavenly tune" (71–72), and such ameliorating guidance is his own function. He mediates between the highest harmony and its impact on the material world; indeed that harmony works through the Genius

---

8. The phrase is reminiscent of the joyful wantonness of the music in *L'Allegro,* ll. 136–44, or the fruitful wantoning of the unfallen Paradise in *Paradise Lost* V.294–97.

whose "puissant words and murmurs made to bless" carry to his plants the healing music of the spheres.

The Genius' relation to the masquers parallels his relation to the plants. Once more he is a mediator—this time between the divine light of the Countess and the shepherds, whose opening song shows them puzzled and awed by the "unparallel'd" beauty before them.[9] His guidance as he brings the shepherds to the Countess is again connected with words and music: he chants, "Follow me as I sing, / And touch the warbled string" (86–87). The pairing of song and instrument repeats a formula frequent in the minor poems and reflects the common Renaissance belief that words and music together appeal to the two aspects of man, music to the affections and words to the rational intellect. Together they unite the divided self and raise one to an apprehension of the divine harmony that the Genius hears at night. A famous passage in *The Reason of Church Government* states that the offices of the poet are, among others, "to inbreed and cherish in a great people the seeds of virtue and public civility, to allay the perturbations of the mind and set the affections in right tune, to celebrate in glorious and lofty hymns the throne and equipage of God's almightiness, and what he works" (Hughes, p. 669). Emblematically the Genius of the Wood does just this: he has come himself to know the light of truth and leads the shepherds to it with his song. The Genius' characteristic ties with the earth have now gained a metaphorical resonance and extend to the lower part of human nature. In the hands of the poet-Genius, the music which failed to redeem all Nature in the *Nativity Ode* touches the individual and leads him to the light of truth.

Comus is Milton's most elaborate discussion of the nature of Nature but it is concerned with the nature of poetry as well: once more genii link the two concerns. But the treatment of the guardian spirit here is more complex than it is in *Arcades,* for instead of one genius there are three: the Attendant Spirit, Comus,

9. The opening song of the masquers comes when they first see the goddess and attempt to describe her. All their experience, however, is pagan and their models are insufficient to illuminate her true nature. The shepherds are a little like the wood-inhabitants of the First Book of the *Faerie Queene,* unable to comprehend Una (*F.Q.* I.vi.13–19). Their song ends in uncertainty: "Who had thought this clime had held / A deity so unparallel'd?" (24–25) The Genius comes forward to help them in their awed confusion.

and Sabrina. Although Comus is the spirit of a particular wood, he and the Attendant Spirit derive most of their significance from the tradition of the two personal genii, as A. Kent Heiatt has suggested.[10] They do not fit the demonological pattern exactly, of course; they have not been with the Lady from birth and the Attendant Spirit clearly feels that his is an emergency trip. But Milton stresses the traditional opposition by giving them several common characteristics. Both are guides allegorically disguised as shepherds; both can use the incantatory tetrameter couplets that the strictly human characters do not employ; both are masters of words. In a recent book on Milton as a critic of his own poetic language Christopher Grose remarks that Comus opposes the Attendant Spirit as a "false" rhetorician opposes a true one.[11] More specifically, both are poets, masters of song and music, and their opposition dramatizes the use and abuse of "adjuring verse" (858).

Both are associated with gates. The traditional identification of the genius with the "porter" or gatekeeper enables Milton to stress the genius' function as a mediator here: the poetry of each genius *is* the gate into his realm. Milton invokes the porter tradition in the first line of *Comus* when the Attendant Spirit announces that

> Before the starry threshold of *Jove's* court
> My mansion is . . .
>
> (1–2)

In other words, the Attendant Spirit lives in the porter's lodge; he is the figure who opens the door, leading the blest to the saintly seats he describes later in his speech. While a simple identification of the Attendant Spirit with St. Peter would be overly limiting, it is worth remembering Milton's conscious association in *Lycidas* and elsewhere between the good poet and the good priest. Both are "shepherds" who guide the erring soul back to the path of truth.

Comus' palace also has gates, and their function suggests the significance of the lady's temptation. Attempting to soothe her, he asks:

> Why are you vext, Lady? why do you frown?
> Here dwell no frowns, nor anger, from these gates

---

10. "Milton's Comus," pp. 314–16.
11. Christopher Grose, *Milton's Epic Process* (New Haven, 1973), pp. 85–93.

> Sorrow flies far: See, here be all the pleasures
> That fancy can beget on youthful thoughts,
> When the fresh blood grows lively, and returns
> Brisk as the *April* buds in Primrose-season.
> (666–71)

Comus presides over another seemingly blest realm, a place from which sorrow is absent. He offers the Lady a world of undivided pleasure. And despite the sexual suggestion of the language, the primary powers of the "precious cordial" stimulate not the body but the imagination. It contains "all the pleasures / That fancy can beget on youthful thoughts." Comus may simply be saying "anything you want," but the language is more precise than that. Comus offers the Lady the pleasures of an ungoverned fancy, an imagination that lacks all rational control. The castle into which he has led her is a place of soporific illusion, created by a poetry which keeps the mind occupied with pleasant images, never allowing it to see beyond the words to the Word of God. Comus speaks of this music when he mentions his mother Circe who would

> take the prison'd soul,
> And lap it in *Elysium*
> (256–57)

with her deadening, pleasurable song. The opposition of Comus and the Attendant Spirit thus articulates the opposition between two kinds of poetry: a false and self-centered verse, playing with the tangles of Neaera's hair, and a poetry whose art awakens the soul to look beyond itself to the harmonious order of God.

Comus is a false poet, but he is more. Like many of the figures in Spenser's allegory—and Spenser is Milton's primary model and reference in *Comus*—Comus embodies in himself several distinct but associated concepts, not all of which are operative simultaneously. The world into which he would incorporate the Lady is founded on a series of "per-versions," turnings-aside from God; false poetry is only the most literary representative of these. He is heir of the instinctual god Bacchus, and as such he is the spokesman for the sexual drives which are part of the Lady's own nature. He is also the ruler of a libertine world, a Nature whose only end is to "please and sate the curious taste" (714). The temptations of the "cordial julip" are thus at once sexual and philosophical and literary: they join in a fundamental self-centeredness, a refusal to use God's creation and God's talents for anything but narcissistic self-gratification.

The Lady's surprising immobility after she has defeated Comus in argument has been accounted for by Richard Neuse, who suggests that it is in part her own will that keeps her immobile.[12] Comus embodies, among other things, the animal nature that gives the Lady all power of motion. When she overcomes Comus in argument, reason and passion oppose one another in deadlock: neither can vanquish the other sufficiently to allow the Lady to act. It is to resolve this fruitless opposition that Sabrina arises, not to suppress Comus further, but to reconcile the energies that he represents with the guidance offered by the Attendant Spirit. Like Comus, Sabrina is a genius, probably the first feminine genius in English literature.[13] She is not a personal genius but a spirit of place, the goddess of the Severn river. Like the genii of the earlier poems, she works in twilight and is described caring for her plants (843–47) in language which recalls the self-description of the Genius of *Arcades*. But while Sabrina is distinct from Comus she is also associated with him. When the Attendant Spirit invokes her, he calls on her in the name of the nymphs and sirens who are part of Comus' world and, like the genius-tempter, she heals with "precious vial'd liquors" (847). Yet in bridled, purified form, she represents the impulses that Comus embodies. Whereas Comus remembers the sirens whose songs would lap the prisoned soul in a false Elysium, Sabrina's sirens are harmless and playful. The attendant Spirit calls on her by

12. "Metamorphosis and Symbolic Action in *Comus*," *ELH* 34 (1967), 49–64; reprinted in *Critical Essays on Milton from ELH* (Baltimore, 1969), pp. 87–102.

13. I speak of Sabrina as a genius because she is described in terms which recall those characterizing the Genius of *Arcades*. In doing so I am, however, departing from classical usage. Genii are traditionally male; Roy A. Swanson has pointed out to me that the female equivalent of a genius would, in classical times, have been a Juno (see Pauly and Wissowa, eds., *Real-Encyclopädie*, VII, 1157). Milton gains several advantages from making the reconciling genius a woman, the most obvious of which is the similarity established between Sabrina and the Lady. Like the Lady, Sabrina has been an innocent and persecuted virgin, and she has now attained the earthly equivalent of the "sainted seats" (11) to which the Lady's virtue will lead her. Sabrina thus becomes an image of the reconciling harmony which the Lady symbolically learns. She is the supreme mediator of the masque, at once human, natural, and divine.

> the Songs of *Sirens* sweet
> By dead *Parthenope's* dear tomb,
> And fair *Ligea's* golden comb,
> Wherewith she sits on diamond rocks
> Sleeking her soft alluring locks . . .
>   (878–82)

Parthenope's death (according to one version of the myth the result of her disappointment at her failure to destroy Ulysses) is here divorced from its violence and her tomb becomes a "dear" landmark. Sabrina's liquors, unlike Comus' transforming cordial, bring true healing.

Sabrina rises in response to the Attendant Spirit's invocation, his employment of "warbled Song" with the addition of "some adjuring verse" (854–58). The musical guidance of this scene recapitulates in a more complex fashion the musical conversion of *Arcades*. Through the mingled voice and verse of the invocation, Comus' liberal energies reappear in the purified form of Sabrina—herself halfway between the otherworldliness of the Attendant Spirit and the earthiness of Comus. It is fitting that Sabrina should be the deity of a river flowing through wild Wales and yet "crowned" (934) with the cities of civilized Britain.

Although, like *Arcades, Lycidas* dramatizes a conversion from pagan to Christian pastoral and links its investigation of Nature with an examination of poetry, it nonetheless differs from the earlier poems.[14] The questioning is harsher and more radical: at times the created world appears "monstrous" and poetry no more than a helpless and melodious tear. Both *Arcades* and *Comus* assume that it is "natural" for the goodness of the world to harmonize with that of the Creator, and even the *Nativity Ode* envisions winds, waves, and stars peacefully rejoicing in Christ's incarnation. But *Lycidas* concerns itself with a Nature subject to death, the primary result of the Fall. The sounding seas have been instrumental in Lycidas' death, and this suggests that Nature

14. The seminal essays on Nature and poetry in *Lycidas* are those of Isabel MacCaffrey ("*Lycidas:* The Poet in a Landscape," in *The Lyric and Dramatic Milton,* ed. Joseph H. Summers [New York, 1965], pp. 65–92) and Jon Lawry (" 'Eager Thought': Dialectic in *Lycidas,*" *PMLA* 57 [1962], 27–32). See also the recent treatments of the poem in Grose, *Epic Process,* pp. 94–119, and in Donald M. Friedman, "*Lycidas:* The Swain's Paideia," *Milton Studies* 3 (1971), 3–34.

herself may be governed by malevolent or indifferent forces—the
"blind *Fury* with th'abhorred shears" (75) or the unpropitious
stars on which Hippotades puts final blame. The poet's own deep
fear of an early death underlies all other questions: How can there
be justice and order in a world which interrupts a dedicated life
before it can come to fruition?

The question is all the more urgent because we know so little. In
the *Nativity Ode* the speaker describes the events surrounding the
incarnation with prophetic certainty; in the *Epitaphium Damonis*
Thyrsis grieves for his friend's loss but he feels no need to wonder
how or why it happened. The swain of *Lycidas,* by contrast, lacks
the most essential facts: Where is his friend's body? Who or what
is responsible for the death? The answers he receives are indirect
and unsatisfying: Triton hears nothing from the winds and waves
while Aeolus blames the ship built under the influence of malevolent stars—thus exonerating the creation of one level by
blaming it at a higher one. Roy Daniells has drawn attention to
the frustration of the swain's questioning as a "mannerist" trait,[15]
but the obliquity has a thematic function as well. The unclarities
of the poem, of which St. Peter's mysterious "two-handed engine"
is the most famous, suggest how difficult it is to obtain any
rational certainty about last things.

The sheer number of mediating figures in the central section of
the poem—Apollo, Neptune, Triton, Aeolus, St. Peter—suggests
how difficult it is to perceive the truth "directly." Even Neptune,
the main representative of Nature in the poem, is himself at one
remove, represented in turn by Triton and Aeolus. The Spenserian
figure of Camus epitomizes the limits of the fallen intellect. He is
the second figure in the progression from Neptune (the material
world) to St. Peter (Spirit) and his association with Cambridge
suggests that he embodies the powers of human reason. But he
moves slowly and his only utterance is a baffled question: " 'Ah!
Who hath reft' (quoth he) 'my dearest pledge?' " (107). His hat is
covered with "figures dim" (105), perhaps a reminder of the
obscurity of all knowledge on "this dim spot / Which men call
Earth" (*Comus,* 5–6). The other sign on his hat, "Like to that
sanguine flower inscrib'd with woe" (106), is an emblem of the
sorrowful change that characterizes life on earth. While the

15. *Milton, Mannerism and Baroque* (Toronto, 1963), pp. 37–50.

metamorphosis that ends the Hyacinth myth may look forward to
the triumphant transformations later in the poem, the immediate
context of the line stresses only sorrow and unnecessary loss.
Hyacinth, like Lycidas, died young because of accident or the
malice of a minor god.

If Nature is corrupt, poetry seems helpless. *Lycidas* makes
explicit the question inherent in many pastoral elegies, whether
poetry can do anything in the face of death.[16] The opposition of
death and poetry is announced in the opening paragraph:

> He must not float upon his wat'ry bier
> Unwept, and welter to the parching wind,
> Without the meed of some melodious tear.
> (12–14)

The making of the poem is a formal—indeed a quasi-ritual—act
and opposes the aimless "weltering" of Lycidas' body. The "meed"
of poetic praise attempts to compensate for the untimely in-
terruption of Lycidas' life. Yet the power of such praise is limited:
it cannot celebrate actions that Lycidas has not lived to perform.
And even such consolation as poetic celebration can give will soon
be undercut when Apollo denigrates earthly fame in favor of
Heaven's praise. What is the use of poetic "meed" if the true
reward for virtuous action comes from the "perfect witness of all-
judging *Jove*" (82)?

The swain does for a moment raise the possibility of a poetry
which is more than a "melodious tear" in his references to the
Druid bards and to Orpheus. These are poet-magicians whose
"charms" remold the world according to their wishes. It is with
this view of poetry as evoking and controlling the forces of the
earth that the swain begins to call on the nymphs who should have
protected their bard. But this version of poetry as magic is rapidly
dismissed as delusion: "Ay me, I fondly dream!" (56). Even
Orpheus, for all his "enchanting" power, is unable to defend
himself against the fury of the bacchantes. The fantasy of a poetry
which controls Nature yields to a despondent vision of human
helplessness, just as the swain's later evasion in the catalogue of

16. The helplessness of poetry in *Lycidas* is a primary theme of Fred J. Nichols,
" 'Lycidas,' 'Epitaphium Damonis': The Empty Dream, the Failed Song," in *Acta Con-
ventus Neo-Latini Lovaniensis,* ed. J. IJsewijn and E. Kessler (Munich, 1973), pp. 445–
52.

flowers will give way to the terrible image of Lycidas' body tossed about by the waves.

The possibility of a poetry which is neither all-powerful nor entirely helpless does not begin to emerge until St. Peter's speech. Apollo, for all the Christian promise of his words, seems more concerned with good *men* than with good *poets*. St. Peter, on the contrary, speaks of pastors who are singers as well. Indeed, one function of the Christian pastoral idiom of his speech is to bring together the two aspects of pastoral life—herding and singing—that the swain treats separately.[17] True pastoral singing *is* the proper tending of sheep, for singing is spiritual feeding. The bad pastors are bad not because they spend time in song but because their songs are "lean and flashy" (123), externally showy but devoid of nourishing doctrine. Bad pastors are concerned, like Comus, with the goods of this world but they miss the symbolic meaning of those goods. They gorge themselves on the material "feast" but they leave their flocks to starve spiritually or to be devoured by the Roman Catholic "Wolf with privy paw" (128). Peter's diatribe thus faces the world's fallen state and implicitly offers a remedy for it. The singing of the faithful shepherd may not perform miracles but it can begin to cure the sickness of human sinfulness. Further, in Peter's speech the self-centered element in the swain's questioning has been transcended: poetic power is not used here for self-preservation but for the protection and nourishment of others. The substitution of Christian for pagan pastoral thus places both the poet and his singing at the service of God. This conversion is suggested at the opening of the passage where St. Peter is introduced as the "Pilot of the *Galilean* lake" (109). The reference is to Matthew 4:12–22, where Peter and his fellow fishermen first witness Christ's miracles and become fishers of men. Like the pastoral idiom in which he speaks, St. Peter has been converted.

The swain's retreat from the "dread voice" of Peter's anger and his attempt to "dally" with "false surmise" in the subsequent flower-catalogue has been fully discussed by Donald Friedman

17. In classical pastoral, singing and herding are often opposed occupations: too much attention to song can involve neglecting one's sheep. See Virgil, *Eclogues* VII.17 and IX.61–67. One of the *topoi* of Elizabethan pastoral is the shepherd who bewails his grief in song and forgets about his sheep. See Spenser, "January," in *The Shepheards Calendar,* and Milton's own *Epitaphium Damonis* with its refrain "Ite domum impasti, domino iam non vacat, agni."

and others.[18] The reversal of the poem begins when the swain realizes that he has been dallying and, in a profound depression, envisions Lycidas' body at the mercy of the waves. At this moment, when things seem worst, the swain's perspective begins to change. He resigns himself to the uncertainties surrounding Lycidas' death, admitting by the conscious surmises of the passage ("where'er . . . Whether . . . whether . . .") that the body is beyond finding. Yet for the first time in the poem his concern for his friend appears completely unselfish. Until this moment Lycidas' fate has been an example of what might happen to *him;* hence his mind turns rapidly from Lycidas' funeral to his own (19–24) and from Lycidas' incomplete career to his own (64–76). Now, in praying for Lycidas, the swain moves beyond the largely self-centered inquiry of the earlier part of the poem. Most important in turning to prayer the swain leaves his earlier pastoral song and steps forth as a prophet. The style heightens, and after the intimate and local catalogue of flowers, the poet's vision enlarges to include all England in its relation to Namancos and Bayona's hold: his perspective approximates that of Michael or St. Peter.

In this new prophetic role the swain is able in the next lines to encourage other men with a divinely-sent vision: "Weep no more, woeful Shepherds, weep no more . . ." (165). The grim opening of the poem, "Yet once more, O ye Laurels, and once more / Ye Myrtles brown . . ." (1–2) here finds its resolution.[19] The pagan vision of a world of endlessly repeated cycles in which there is always *more* has already been challenged by St. Peter's apocalyptic prophecy of the two-handed engine which "Stands ready to smite once and smite no more" (131). Time will have an ending and with that ending a meaning and purpose. Already the swain can now see Lycidas, who has transcended the natural cycle and who stands where angels can "wipe the tears *for ever* from his eyes" (181; italics mine).

The swain has adopted the mode of Christian pastoral which St. Peter has used, and the climax of this transformed pastoral

18. See Friedman, "The Swain's Paideia," pp. 15–22; MacCaffrey, "Poet in a Landscape," pp. 84–85. Several points in this paragraph are made in Friedman's essay.

19. This repetition was brought to my attention by Marshall Brown. Many pastoral elegies have refrains which are discarded or change or take on new meaning when the lament changes to consolation. The effect of "more" in the poem is that of a minimal refrain, crystalizing meaning at crucial moments in the poem (1, 131, 165, 182).

comes in the final revision of the genius-figure that has appeared
in the earlier poems:

> Now *Lycidas,* the Shepherds weep no more;
> Henceforth thou art the Genius of the shore,
> In thy large recompense, and shalt be good
> To all that wander in that perilous flood.
>   (182–85)

In these rich lines the genius, traditionally a local spirit, has been
elevated into a guardian of the whole British shore. Yet the image
of a "Genius of the shore" has a resonance which is more than
national: Lycidas has become a spirit guiding all those wandering
through the uncertain waters of this world. The metaphor is
typically Spenserian, though it derives ultimately from biblical
typology. One "shore" which would have been familiar to the
readers of the poem is surely the promised land, the country of
God's faithful. The final shore is not of this world.

Yet why should Lycidas, as distinct from other good men,
become a genius? Surely the translation to heaven would have
been an adequate reward. The lines suggest that Lycidas will continue, even after death, to exert a benevolent power over those
left in this world. That power is, I think, exerted through Milton's
poem. Poetry converts and does so, according to the familiar
Sidneyan dictum, by example. Lycidas' image in this poem
exemplifies not heroic achievement but the better fortitude of a
dedicated service which lasted as long as the great taskmaster saw
fit, a service which is eventually given its just reward. The
example of Lycidas in the poem thus takes the place of Henry
King in its power to stir the reader to virtuous action. And in this
final apotheosis the earthly fame which Apollo has discounted
gains a new value. Lycidas' glory will serve not to immortalize
himself but to praise God. It will justify the ways of God to men.
And in this transcendence of self lies the answer to the deepest fear
of the poem, that of untimely death. All deaths are timely: God
fulfills himself in many ways, as he has in the case of Lycidas. It is
for the individual Christian to submit to the divine will which,
ever unknowable, brings the seemingly fruitless accidents of
history to final fruition. The theme is a familiar one throughout
Milton's poetry and is implicit in Lycidas' transformation and the
swain's difficult progress.

In the last English poems of the 1645 volume Milton's use of genii begins to change. Neither Sabrina nor Lycidas is originally a nature-god; they are Christian innocents who die and are resurrected to serve in their new functions. Sabrina, fleeing from her revengeful stepmother, "Commended her fair innocence to the flood" (831) of the Severn and, touched by Nereus' ambrosial oils, undergoes a "quick immortal change" to become goddess of the river (824–42). Lycidas also undergoes a death by drowning and a resurrection which makes him into a genius. As Milton becomes increasingly self-conscious in his use of genii, the model of Christ as the true poet-genius becomes increasingly explicit. Christ as *the* mediator between God and man partakes of both worlds and enables others to do so: in him the Word is made flesh and through him fallen mankind can attain to blessedness. Christ is also the model for the poet-orator, preaching the gospel to the sinful, using figurative language in the parables, healing and raising to life by words.[20] In *At a Solemn Music* the speaker accords to the marriage of Voice and Verse the divine power to pierce "Dead things with inbreath'd sense" (4). This revival is accomplished by the process dramatized in *Comus* and *Arcades,* in which the divine harmony creates its counterpart in the human soul. Thus the genius who is, in the *Nativity Ode,* forced to flee the coming of Christ becomes, by the time of *Lycidas,* a figure modeled on Christ himself. In *Lycidas,* indeed, the genius has lost most of his "pagan" attributes. He is a national rather than a local spirit and has become an abiding example of the dedicated Christian.

In the works after the 1645 *Poems,* the genius is banished once more. There are, strictly speaking, no genii in *Paradise Lost, Paradise Regained,* or *Samson Agonistes,* while the later prose makes little use of the figure.[21] The disappearance of the genius reflects two related developments in Milton's thought: an in-

20. Joseph Anthony Wittreich, Jr., comments on Milton's use, in his prose writings, of Christ as the model of the poet-orator in " 'The Crown of Eloquence': The Figure of the Orator in Milton's Prose Works," in *Achievements of the Left Hand: Essays on the Prose of John Milton,* ed. Michael Lieb and John Shawcross (Amherst, 1974), esp. pp. 8–11.

21. Most of the prose references to "genius" come in the early familiar epistles and in the sixth and seventh prolusions. There are, however, a flurry of references to genii in the *Second Defense* and the *Defense of Himself.* In the former Milton refers to Cromwell as the "tutelary genius of liberty" (Hughes, ed., *Complete Poems and Major Prose,* p. 835), but in most cases he uses the word in the more modern sense of "native intellectual power."

creased distrust of pagan myth and an intensified awareness of the spiritual danger, for fallen man, of attempting to locate the sacred in created things.[22] The double change can be seen in the catalogue of pagan deities in *Paradise Lost,* so much more severe than its equivalent in the *Nativity Ode.* These figures are evil primarily because they seduce men from the *invisible* glory of the creator to worship brutish *images* (I 365–73). The temptations of the later poems all involve mistaking image for truth, external symbol for internal essence—whether the external value be found in an apple, or worldly power, or physical strength. In *Paradise Lost* the flood reduces the mount of Paradise to a sterile island to prove that "God attributes to place / No sanctity" (XI.836–37). A natural god cannot survive in such a context.

But the promptings that the early poetry associates with genii are not, of course, abandoned: they are identified with the breath of God as it works in the elect. When Samson cries that his "genial spirits droop" (594) he is admitting that he has lost the divine impulse that has previously enabled him to act, and when he begins to feel some "rousing motions" in himself (1382), those genial spirits have begun to work once more. In *Paradise Lost* the internal guide and teacher has become the poet's muse. The name of this mediating spirit is never certain, just as its nature remains beyond precise definition: it fuses characteristics of a Christianized Urania, Divine Sapience, and God's own light. The inward nature of the muse is most fully described in the prologue to Book III, where the divine light that it brings contrasts with the light of Nature that the poet has lost. The connection between a genius and a muse is already apparent in *Il Penseroso,* where the melancholy man has a "strange mysterious dream" and wakes hearing sweet music in a wood presided over by a benevolent guardian spirit (131–54). The divine muse of *Paradise Lost* also visits the waking speaker with "Harmonious numbers" (III.38) but this muse is not a spirit of place at all: its realm is the inner temple of the human heart and unlike the Genius of the Wood it is all light. The prompting spirit has become unequivocally internalized, leaving its pagan and worldly past behind.

---

22. Two discussions of this concern in the later poetry can be found in Grose, *Milton's Epic Process,* and Michael McCanles, *Dialectic in Renaissance Literature* (Berkeley, 1975).

The Singer and his Song
in the Prologues of Paradise Lost

ROGER H. SUNDELL

The prologues to Books I, III, VII, and IX of *Paradise Lost* are separable from the rest of Milton's epic poem. Each prologue is, in a sense, an independent poem and together the four form a single poem that is controlled by a distinctive voice, moves with its own progression, and embodies its own themes and purpose. In short, Milton's prologues cohere as a unit with its own literary integrity.

This is not to say that the prologues are not intimately a part of the epic. Critical commentary on *Paradise Lost* abounds with justifications of them in terms of their functions within the larger poem. The springboard for such justifications is often Samuel Johnson's descriptions of the prologues to Books III, VII, and IX as "short digressions" that "might doubtless be spared," yet as "superfluities" sufficiently beautiful to be retained.[1] E. M. W. Tillyard, for example, finds "Milton's opening . . . at once the prologue to the whole poem and the prologue to the first movement."[2] Each of the later prologues, he contends, marks the transition between major stages ("movements") of the poem's story. In "The Function of the Prologues in *Paradise Lost*," John Diekhoff adopts Tillyard's "justification" and adds his own. All of the prologues, he argues, provide, at critical points in the logical progression of the poem, "ethical proof"—"the demonstration of

---

1. Samuel Johnson, "Life of Milton," in *Lives of the English Poets* (Oxford, 1905), I, 175.
2. E. M. W. Tillyard, *Milton* (London, 1934), p. 237.

[Milton's] fitness to speak on the subject in hand."[3] Anne
Davidson Ferry's *Milton's Epic Voice* (1963) has influenced much
of the subsequent commentary on the prologues. She describes
their principal function as the invention of an appropriate
narrative voice. "The identity and characteristic tone" of that
voice are created and defined in the prologues, and they are
"sustained throughout the epic and control our interpretation of
its meaning."[4] Given the enormous critical popularity of point-of-
view studies during the past two decades, it is not surprising that
commentators have continued to emphasize "the figure of the
poet" and its relationships to the reader and to the author. Stanley Fish's influential *Surprised by Sin* takes that figure to a
rhetorical extreme in a combined heroic and ministerial role. The
speaker is Milton, prophet and Socratic teacher; the fit audience is
fallen man; the poem is essentially a teaching mechanism, "an
instrumentality of divinity."[5] William Kerrigan, whose commentary on the "invocations" in *The Prophetic Milton* is the most
extended to date and, perhaps, the most searching, narrows the
poem's audience to an exclusive "group of solitary outcasts" as he
argues that "the inspired poet has suffered from a conspiracy of
tactful disinterest" on the part of critics who have refused to
acknowledge a Milton who "believed himself a prophet" and, as
in the epic prologues, "spoke as a prophet . . . [whose] belief in
intimate impulse and divine favor sustained him through most of
his life."[6]

These citations are only a sampling from a large body of
valuable critical commentary on Milton's prologues.[7] That

3. John S. Diekhoff, "The Function of the Prologues in *Paradise Lost,*" *PMLA* 57
(1942), 698.

4. Anne Davidson Ferry, *Milton's Epic Voice: The Narrator in* Paradise Lost (Cambridge, Mass., 1967), pp. 20–22.

5. Stanley E. Fish, *Surprised by Sin: The Reader in* Paradise Lost (New York, 1967), p.
206.

6. William Kerrigan, *The Prophetic Milton* (Charlottesville, Va., 1974), pp. 180, 4, 6.

7. Among other recent studies are four that focus variously on the figure of the poet as
creator. In *The Dialectics of Creation* (Amherst, Mass., 1970), Michael Lieb explores the
range of the speaker's experience as a mythic, heroic journey made possible by the muse
(pp. 37–55). Christopher Grose, in *Milton's Epic Process* (New Haven, 1973), discusses
the "invocations" as revealing the conditions of the poem's "achievement" and "the
discreteness . . . of poem and process" (pp. 245–63). More pertinent to my own study is
Roger B. Rollin's "*Paradise Lost:* 'Tragical-Comical-Historical-Pastoral' " (*Milton Studies*
5 [1973], 3–37). Rollin describes in Milton's prologues the "monodrama of Milton's

commentary reveals a various and healthy responsiveness to passages that most readers of the epic remember and love. It also reveals the tendency on the part of critics to approach the prologues in ways that blur significant distinctions between them and the narrative they introduce. Samuel Johnson's judgment of the final three prologues as justifiable only in terms of their inherent beauty is no longer acceptable; but it does rightly emphasize the value of examining all of them as passages whose function is in part independent from the poem's main story.

When viewed as an independent poem, Milton's prologues reveal remarkable coherence. Each one is, of course, a single verse paragraph, placed conspicuously in an introductory position. And there are, in all four of them, three main subjects that recur—the poet, his muse, and the poem. The opening prologue introduces all three of these subjects; each of the others focuses on and develops one of them. The figure of the poet is most fully explored in the prologue to III, which is sometimes described as the "most personal."[8] Urania—"the meaning, not the name"—dominates the opening of Book VII. Book IX's prologue deals mainly with the nature of the heroic poem. While this thematic progress is not exclusive (there are personal notes in VII and IX, for example, and references to the muse in III and IX), the focus on a single subject is prominent and purposeful, and it indicates a degree of system and coherence that most scholars overlook.

Close observation of the four prologues reveals as well significant differences in their design. R. W. Condee has shown that the opening of Book I follows a "formalized" pattern (*principium, invocatio, initium,* etc.) that combines Homeric and Virgilian forms of introduction; the speaker not only asks the muse to sing, but also requests inspiration for himself.[9] In the familiar epic manner, central questions follow the requests: "Say

---

narrator" and anticipates my own focus on the evolving, changing character of Milton's speaker. Finally, William G. Riggs, in *The Christian Poet in Paradise Lost* (Berkeley, 1972), attempts to show the presence of Milton as Christian poet throughout the "total design" of the epic. His study is valuable, though it does not include a systematic study of the prologues, but rather refers to them selectively.

8. See, for example, John Carey and Alastair Fowler, eds., *The Poems of John Milton* (London, 1968), p. 559.

9. R. W. Condee, "The Formalized Openings of Milton's Epic Poems," *Journal of English and Germanic Philology* 50 (1951), 503.

first . . . what cause / Mov'd our Grand Parents . . . to fall off / From thir Creator?" and "Who first seduc'd them?"[10] The immediate answer to the second question ("Th' infernal Serpent") abruptly ends the process of seeking or generating an appropriate narrative voice and begins the narrative proper. The same pattern of invocation ("Descend from Heav'n *Urania*," "Return me to my Native Element," and "So fail not thou, who thee implores") and interrogation ("what ensu'd . . . when *Raphaël* . . . had forewarn'd / *Adam?*") occurs in Book VII. And that same prominent separation of the voice in the prologue from the voice of the epic narrator occurs where the narrative begins (VII.50–51): "He with his consorted *Eve* / The story heard attentive." Thus the prologues to I and VII, the beginning and midpoints of the epic, share a formalized manner of initiating the story, a point seldom noticed by commentators.[11] The second "opening" of the epic emphasizes its bipartite structure (underscored as well by the phrase "Half yet remains unsung"). It further emphasizes the shift in the narrative from supernatural and otherworldly affairs to events centered on man and earth. And it also draws attention self-consciously both to the speaker's need for renewed inspiration and to his apprehensions regarding his success and the poem's. Much the same effect results from the multiple invocations in *Lycidas,* where the "uncouth Swain" reveals his own apprehensions and also some sense of inadequacy by reinvoking the pastoral muses following the "interruptions" of his song first by Phoebus' strain "of a higher mood" and second by the "dread voice" of St. Peter.

While the prologues to I and VII are markedly similar in design, the other two are unique. In the prologue to III, there is a request for inspiration, but it is not addressed to the Heavenly Muse, although her guidance is acknowledged in the third person ("Taught by the heav'nly Muse to venture down"). Rather, the

10. All quotations of Milton are from John Milton, *Complete Poems and Major Prose,* ed. Merritt Y. Hughes (New York, 1957).

11. The studies by Rollin and Kerrigan (cited above) are among the relatively few that rightly emphasize the distinction between the "initiating" and "narrating" voices in the poem. While Rollin sustains that distinction, Kerrigan tends to blur it deliberately, using the term "narrator" in reference to both the speaker in the prologues and what he calls, in the narrative, the "mingled voice" of narrator and muse (*The Prophetic Milton,* pp. 139–46).

speaker addresses "holy Light" as "Thou" and asks that it "Shine inward." And in this instance, no epic question follows. Aside from the "invocation to Light" and some transitional matter, this prologue is mainly a study of the figure of the poet. In the prologue to IX, there is no invocation at all and only conditional references—again in the third person—to the continuing aid of the muse: "If answerable style I can obtain / Of my Celestial Patroness" and "if all be mine, / Not Hers who brings it nightly to my Ear." Again, the narrative begins without prompting questions, and it begins abruptly (IX.48): "The Sun was sunk." This prologue deals principally with the nature of the poem being composed and with its predecessors. The prologue to IX then is not in any ordinary sense an invocation and the prologue to III does not follow the same pattern of introducing as any of the others. To describe all four prologues as "invocations" over-simplifies passages that appear significantly different both in design and in intent. For the prologues divide into pairs. The first and third are invocations according to a conventional pattern; the second and fourth are, by contrast, in part literary progress reports and in part commentaries on subjects introduced in the opening prologue.

A reading of the prologues in isolation from the story in *Paradise Lost* also reveals their distinctive voice. That voice belongs to a figure of a poet, and it is wise, I suggest, to differentiate it from the voice of the omniscient, editorial narrator, whose functions as teller and interpreter of the story are distinct and whose manner of narrating throughout the poem's twelve books remains relatively consistent, predictable, and, again, distinct. The poet-speaker's voice, however, is not predictable, nor is it uniform in tone. His attitude towards himself and his projected work appears to shift from one prologue to the next. Such shifts suggest the possibility of discovering a speaker who is not the static "blind bard," "inspired poet," or "prophet" posited in most commentary, but rather an objectified and developing character whose experience of creating a sacred epic effects significant changes in himself. The speaker of the prologues does "intrude" during the narrative. But the several apostrophes in Book IV, for example, including its opening call for the "warning voice" of St. John, do not blur at all the distinction between poet-speaker and narrator. Rather, they emphasize the speaker's intense commitment to the "great Argument" and his recognition of its pertinence to himself and his readers.[12]

It is wise, as well, to differentiate the figure of the poet from its creator, Milton. As is frequently noted, they are alike in many respects. But Milton apparently took great pains to distance himself from that figure, and even more from the epic narrator called forth in the prologues. He writes deliberately, of course, in a tradition of "inspired" poet-figures. And, as Robert M. Durling notes, "The dominant convention of the epic is that its narrator is a supernaturally inspired man who transmits a story received from outside himself."[13] Milton's wide range of references and allusions in the prologues to earlier literary works and to other poets and prophets, and the speaker's invocations to multiple sources of inspiration all emphasize the formulaic—almost mythic—nature of that poet-speaker, as well as his uniqueness. Roger Rollin succinctly argues that we know about the created character, the persona for John Milton, "only what John Milton the poet wishes us to know and when he wishes us to know it."[14] Most of the "biographical" passages are, in fact, fairly vague or even obscure. The reference to "evil times" and "evil tongues" in Prologue VII, for example, can lead only to conjecture. The references to blindness clustered in Prologue III are rarely precise and generally in tune with traditional conceptions of such blind poets and prophets as Homer and Tiresias. And, as I suggest later, they serve well the purpose of characterization. Adding to the distance between author and speaker are many of the characteristics of language that distinguish one voice from another—diction, syntax, rhythm, intonation, tone and so forth—and that define the vocal integrity of the prologues and appear to be shaped from them alone.[15] Finally, if, as I will argue, the figure of the

12. For contrasting discussion, see Kerrigan, *The Prophetic Milton,* pp. 150–52 and passim.

13. Robert M. Durling, *The Figure of the Poet in Renaissance Epic* (Cambridge, Mass., 1965), p. 9.

14. Rollin, *"Paradise Lost,"* p. 30.

15. There is need for a thorough comparative study of voices in the poem, including those of the prologues' speaker and the epic narrator. Most work that emphasizes elements of style is not thus comparative, and most fails to relate distinguishing elements of style to specific characters. David Daiches' extended reading of Prologue I, "The Opening of *Paradise Lost,*" in *The Living Milton,* ed. Frank Kermode (London, 1963), pp. 55–69, offers a number of excellent stylistic observations, but not with the intent nor the effect of defining a distinctive voice therein. And Donald Davie's study of "Syntax and Music in

poet is seen not as a static, but as a changing character involved in a progression of events, it is the more sensible to leave Milton himself removed far enough from that figure for him to be able to manipulate it according to his best artistic judgment and for us to avoid the temptations to narrow its "identity" and impose interpretations and judgments not clearly or necessarily pertinent to the poem's text.

Like Herbert's "Jordan" poems and Marvell's "The Coronet," Milton's prologues comprise a poem about making a sacred poem. But Milton develops his poet-figure intermittently and gradually, prologue by prologue, with remarkable subtlety and far more complexity than in those lyrics. In the commentary to follow, I will suggest a tonal progression in the voice of that figure which moves from cautious yet conspicuous confidence to something like presumption, then to apprehensiveness, and finally to regained confidence, tested and matured. Such designations of tone inevitably oversimplify the complex of attitudes expressed in substantial passages of good verse. But they do help, still, to describe the crucial affective element of language and thus to define here the speaker's relationships with his subject and audience. The "personal" experience of the speaker, thus reflected in shifts of tone, appears to coincide with and result from the making of the sacred epic. His stance as a poet—the self-image he projects, both in relation to his audience (muse or reader) and to his poem—is proper at the outset, flawed during the process of creation, and finally modified appropriately at the end. In short, Milton's epic speaker becomes the figure of a Christian whose service is singing and whose singing is an adventurous and finally successful trial of his own virtue.[16]

Paradise Lost," in the same volume (pp. 70–84), contributes some pertinent comments on the voice in Prologue III. Similarly, Christopher Ricks's excellent "defense" of the poet's style in *Milton's Grand Style* (Oxford, 1963) contains valuable cross-referencing of diction in Prologues I and IX (pp. 28–29 and 69–72), while Wayne Shumaker explores most interestingly, yet briefly, "affective tonality" in the poem's opening six lines (*Unpremeditated Verse* [Princeton, 1967], pp. 60–64). The study of voice in Milton's epic is thus unsystematic and limited. My own work here focuses on changing tone as it reveals changing character in the prologues, but it is necessarily limited thereto.

16. Some of the recent studies (those, for example, by Riggs, Rollin, and Kerrigan) suggest a similar view, but Rollin alone focuses steadily on the progressive and separate development of the speaker in the prologues. His treatment is suggestive, but very brief; its emphasis is on "dramatic" elements, whereas mine is on character change and tone. We differ, as well, in many points of interpretation and in a number of our conclusions, especially regarding Prologues III and IX.

The exposition of the poet-speaker begins with statements that
seem ambitious and confident to an extreme:

> I thence
> Invoke thy aid to my advent'rous Song
> That with no middle flight intends to soar
> Above th' *Aonian* Mount, while it pursues
> Things unattempted yet in Prose or Rhyme.
> (I.12–15)

and

> What in me is dark
> Illumine, what is low raise and support:
> That to the highth of this great Argument
> I may assert Eternal Providence,
> And justify the ways of God to men.
> (I.22–26)

The poetry here is powerful and grand. The ambitions expressed
in it are extraordinary. But the figure of the poet conveys these
ambitions with more tact and caution than is always recognized.
Though he never describes the creative process in detail, he does
indicate here its cooperative nature, and this point is crucial for
determining the prologue's tone. The speaker "may assert" and
"justify" if the Spirit he implores hears him and responds with that
illumination and support he seeks. From the Heavenly Muse the
speaker invokes aid to his "advent'rous Song" and it is the personified song, not the speaker, that, so aided, "intends to soar . . .
while it pursues." Even the words "advent'rous," "intends," and
"pursues" all cautiously suggest a tentative process of reaching out
or venturing towards a goal, but not necessarily attaining it. The
speaker is thus acutely aware of the difficulties and uncertainties
of his task, and he takes great pains to convey that awareness. Yet
he speaks both eloquently and forcefully of the poem's "whole
subject," "Man's First Disobedience" and what follows from it.
The "Argument" he has selected is "great." Without hesitation, he
refers to *his* "advent'rous Song" and its exceptional stylistic and
thematic intentions. Ambition and confidence in the opening
prologue are clearly present, but tempered by qualifications, by
declarative sentences with implicit conditional meanings, and by
forthright avowals of personal frailties.

The invocations in this prologue may also seem bold and presumptuous—and to some extent they are. The speaker first addresses the Heavenly Muse who inspired Moses, associating her with visionary power (Oreb), priestly duty (Sinai), and, perhaps, a newly purified or purifying vision (Sion Hill and Siloa's Brook). The powers thus invoked are extraordinary, yet strengthened further when the speaker implores "chiefly Thou O Spirit, that dost prefer / Before all Temples th' upright heart and pure," a plea probably, though not necessarily, to the divine figure most accessible to man, the Son of God.[17] Here is a poet-figure whose song "intends to soar / Above th' *Aonian* Mount," transcending the works of pagan writers, and whose accumulated visionary powers, if granted, provide the authority of both biblical testaments. But the "if" is crucial. The speaker does not demand or assume; rather, he implores. And he does not name his muse with precision, but rather invokes multiple sources (muse and Spirit) allusively. Further, as if recognizing that precise knowledge of the muse is beyond understanding and perhaps forbidden, he provides for alternative dwelling places where he may address that muse and from which the muse, if willing, may grant his requests. The speaker is cautious, then, as he approaches sacred sources for his sacred epic. However bold we find him in the invocations, we should also recognize the care with which he phrases them and a humility implied by his manner of phrasing.

The speaker of the opening prologue is a man who shares "our woe" and our hopes of restoration, who hopes also for that kind of inspiration that helped Moses to speak truly and eloquently, and for illumination and support from a divine Spirit. He will, if his requests are successful, take part in the creation of an "advent'rous Song" that may itself be extraordinary. He presents himself and his ambitious project with remarkable and admirable circumspection.

By the end of the second prologue, the figure of the poet is far more accessible to the reader, and far more complex as a character, than at the end of the first. Most of the prologue to III is about the speaker. He begins and concludes with statements

17. William B. Hunter, Jr., "The Meaning of Holy Light in *Paradise Lost* III," *Modern Language Notes* 74 (1959), 589–92; and "Milton's Urania," *Studies in English Literature* 4 (1964), 35–42.

addressed not to the Heavenly Muse, but to holy or celestial
Light. He revisits "holy Light" (unexpressed in the opening prologue but inherent, perhaps, in its "Spirit") "with bolder wing,"
having been "Taught by the heav'nly Muse to venture" into Hell
and to return. He dwells on his blindness, the "personal" fact that
dominates this passage (but is all but absent in the later
prologues). In spite of his handicap, he remains "Smit with the
love of sacred Song" and he "wanders" day and night through
places associated with such song. Finally he asks that, though
blind, he be given power "to see and tell / Of things invisible to
mortal sight." The speaker thus projects the high ambition of
Prologue I. And he projects much more in this sole extended
commentary on himself.

From line 22 through the end of Prologue II, the speaker dwells
on his blindness. The passage divides, in fact, into two separate
meditations (22–40 and 41–55), each beginning with a lament of
the speaker's blindness: ("but thou / Revisit'st not these eyes, that
roll in vain . . ." and "but not to me returns / Day . . .").
Following each of these laments are passages that provide apparent comfort for the speaker. Yet both passages suggest
problems of a sort the speaker did not experience in the opening
prologue. When he insists, "Yet not the more / Cease I to wander
where the Muses haunt . . ." and proceeds to describe how he
visits Sion "Nightly," he projects an independence and a defen-
siveness not previously encountered. He is acting on his own, with
no reference here to aid or inspiration. He reinforces that mildly
presumptuous stance when he describes feeding on thoughts (his
thoughts, apparently) "that voluntary move / Harmonious numbers." The creative process for the sacred epic now appears focused unduly on the speaker himself.

Even more troublesome are his references to those other poets
and prophets, in lines 32–36:

> nor sometimes forget
> Those other two equall'd with me in Fate,
> So were I equall'd with them in renown,
> Blind *Thamyris,* and blind *Maeonides,*
> And *Tiresias* and *Phineus* Prophets old.

He shares the fate (blindness) of Thamyris and Homer and would
be equalled with them, and perhaps with Tiresias and Phin-

eus, in renown. (The passage does not indicate with any precision whether the speaker always remembers all four ancient figures or whether the latter two are mentioned as examples of renown the speaker hopes to attain.) That renown seems precariously near the worldly fame decried in *Lycidas* as "That last infirmity of Noble mind." Moreover, one must doubt whether the speaker does in fact recall properly the fate of Thamyris, who boasted that he would surpass even the Muses, whereat they angrily maimed him and deprived him, as well, of his memory (*Iliad* II.594–600).[18] The references to the two prophets, both of whose reputations are, by many accounts, tainted, raise similar problems of ambiguity and pertinence.[19]

The second lament on blindness (40–50) is more extended, "personal," and pathetic than the first (22–26). The speaker's loss is a calamity: first he catalogues with increasing intensity those sights that do not return to him. Cloud surrounds him, he adds, and "ever-during dark." He is cut off from "the cheerful ways of men" and, in place of "the Book of knowledge fair," he is

> Presented with a Universal blanc
> Of Nature's works to me expung'd and ras'd,
> And wisdom at one entrance quite shut out.

The lament is powerful, moving, and, I suggest, exaggerated. The speaker is surely not entirely cut off from all cheeerful ways of men, nor from all contact with nature's works. And following the lament, the call for compensating illumination seems less imploring than imperative as the requests accumulate ("Shine inward," "Irradiate," "plant," "Purge and disperse") and focus on the first-person phrase, "that I may see and tell / Of things in-

18. The *Iliad* is the probable source, if not the only pertinent one, for the reference to Thamyris. It is surely a source the speaker in this *epic* poem would not "sometimes forget."

19. Tiresias was blinded, by some accounts, for having divulged secrets of the gods; by others, for having seen Minerva bathing. His fate involved, among other things, seeing but being disbelieved and rejected. As Carey and Fowler note (*The Poems of John Milton*, p. 563), Milton quotes, in his *Second Defense* (*The Works of John Milton*, ed. Frank Allen Patterson et al. [New York, 1931–38], VIII, 64), a description of Tiresias as "strong, but blind and piteous." What, one wonders, does the speaker in the prologues always remember? And Phineus was likewise punished with loss of sight, for having seen and told divine secrets. Milton deliberately challenges that explanation, again in *Second Defense* (Patterson, ed., *Works*, VIII, 63). But his persona in Prologue III fails to clarify the notably ambiguous reference. The entire passage (III.32–36) remains confusing—perhaps the product of an inappropriately self-centered speaker who is indeed confused.

visible to mortal sight." The laments on the speaker's blindness, however powerful and eloquent, embody, then, clear suggestions of disproportionate self-concern, exaggeration, presumption, and even confusion.[20]

Early in this prologue, where the lovely address to Light gives way to transitional matter, the speaker betrays hints of undue self-interest and presumption. It is he who revisits Light. (The active phrase "Thee I revisit" occurs twice, emphasizing his effort and suggesting a hint of bitterness in the subsequent phrase, "but thou / Revisit'st not these eyes.") He revisits Light "with bolder wing," a daring and perhaps slightly damning word in an epic that repeatedly castigates boldness. In Prologue I, the personified song intends to soar; but here the speaker refers to "my flight / Through utter and through middle darkness" as "I sung of *Chaos* and *Eternal Night.*" Not until this point does the speaker acknowledge being "Taught by the heav'nly Muse to venture down." He thus celebrates his own role in a manner not obviously anticipated in the confident but humble stance of Prologue I. And, as Prologue III develops, we find those further evidences discussed earlier of presumption and excessive self-concern. It may be significant that these changes in the speaker occur in the only prologue where, contrary to epic precedent and Aristotelian rule, the persona speaks forcefully and extensively in his own person. By himself and of himself this physically handicapped figure seems ironically flawed in character and most needful of the illumination and grace he has the good sense to request.[21]

The prologue to VII presents another striking change in the speaker. If the dominant personal notes of Prologue III are self-

20. In a superb commentary on "The Theme of *Paradise Lost,* Book III" (*New Essays on Paradise Lost,* ed. Thomas Kranidas [Berkeley, 1971], p. 60), Isabel MacCaffrey discusses this passage on blindness as a preparation of the reader for a movement away from such "temporal pressures and limitations" toward a purer vision and understanding, the powers and limitations of which are revealed in the narrative pattern of Book III. That such a movement occurs is, perhaps, a greater tribute to the forcefulness of the poem's "great Argument" than to any purity of motive on the part of the poet-figure, who dwells so heavily here on those very temporal pressures, personal limitations and, indeed, on both his own achievements and personal ambitions.

21. I am too deeply indebted to J. Max Patrick, especially for suggestions followed in this portion of the essay, to accept his claim of having done only an editor's duty. His aid transcended that obligation.

concern, independence, and presumption, here they shift to contrasting dependence and apprehension. The speaker's preoccupa-
tion shifts drastically from himself to the Heavenly Muse, Urania
in meaning not name. She is the clear focus of his attention in all
but seven and one-half lines (VII.21–28). In the formalized invocation, the speaker asks that she "Descend from Heav'n," then
cautiously questions and clarifies his form of address: "If rightly
thou art call'd. . . . The meaning, not the Name I call." The two
passages (2–4 and 12–20) where the speaker refers to past adventures of singing both emphasize his dependence on her, his
recognition of his own frailty, and his acknowledgement of his
own presumption. In the first passage, the speaker declares his
debt to Urania before he describes his adventure: *"Urania*

> . . . whose Voice divine
> Following, above th' *Olympian* Hill I soar,
> Above the flight of *Pegasean* wing.

The syntactical arrangement here, by contrast with III.13–21,
properly credits the muse. Similarly, in the second passage, the
speaker strategically places his several references to aid and to his
own vulnerability:

> Up *led by thee*
> Into the Heav'n of Heav'ns *I have presum'd*
> An Earthly Guest, and drawn Empyreal Air,
> *Thy temp'ring;* with like safety guided down
> *Return me* to my Native Element:
> *Lest* from this flying Steed *unrein'd,* (as once
> *Bellerophon,* though from a lower Clime)
> Dismounted, on th' *Aleian* Field *I fall*
> *Erroneous there to wander and forlorn.*
> (12–20; my emphases)

The stance of the poet at the outset of this passage is comparatively subdued—even more cautious than in Prologue I and far
more self-effacing than in III.

As the prologue proceeds, the speaker continues to emphasize
his fears of failing and of falling victim to forces outside himself—
evil tongues, darkness, dangers, and solitude. Yet he balances his
apprehensions with the positive recognition that he sings "More

safe . . . with mortal voice, unchang'd / To hoarse or mute,"
with the expression of comfort drawn from the muse's nightly or
morning visits, and, most powerfully, with his confidence that
Urania, unlike the muse of Orpheus, is heavenly, and not "an
empty dream."

Revealing of the apprehension in the speaker's tone are negative
words and phrases that dominate much of the prologue. There are
the striking references to falling ("Lest . . . I fall" and "though
fall'n on evil days, / On evil days though fall'n") and to actual or
potential failures (of Bellerophon, of Calliope, and "So fail not
thou"). Negative words abound in both negative and positive contexts: "unreign'd," "dismounted," "unchang'd / To hoarse or
mute," "Half yet remains unsung," "not rapt above the Pole," "yet
not alone." In such a context the request, "still govern thou my
Song, / *Urania*" is moving, and tactful as well. It properly
acknowledges the speaker's debt to the muse and exposes his
hopes of necessary continued aid. And the request that she find for
the song "fit audience . . . though few" perfectly reflects the
tempered, reasonable stance the poet-figure has now begun to
reassume.

As the prologue to Book IX introduces the final "Tragic" notes
of Man's revolt and disobedience, it also completes the poem
begun in the opening prologue. The last of the three subjects introduced there, the nature of the "advent'rous Song," is the
dominating subject of Prologue IX. And concluded with great
subtlety and skill is the story of the poem's poet-figure.

The final prologue reveals more about the process of poetic
creation than does any other. It focuses on the speaker's primary
role of selecting a subject fit for sacred song ("Since first this
Subject for Heroic Song / Pleas'd me long choosing, and
beginning late" [IX.25–26]). The preceding twelve lines and most
of those that follow defend, explain, and support the choice. It is
with supreme confidence and a touch of humor that the speaker
first faults the arguments of the great classical epics (*Iliad,
Aeneid,* and *Odyssey*) to the advantage of his own. What he must
now relate is a "Sad task, yet argument / Not less but more
Heroic." His descriptions of those earlier heroes and heroics are
reductive. Achilles is "stern" as he pursues hapless Hector "Thrice
Fugitive about *Troy* Wall." Aeneus takes second place to Turnus,

whose "rage" is for Lavinia, "disespous'd" by Aeneus. Odysseus'
adventures   are   reduced   to   complications—entanglements
generated by *"Neptune's* ire or *Juno's."* In the long closing section
(27–47), the speaker describes his personal disinclination to
consider "Wars" as a subject fit for his song. Though wars were
"hitherto the only Argument / Heroic deem'd," he is "not
sedulous by Nature to indite" them, he says at the outset. "Nor,"
he concludes, is he "skill'd nor studious" of them. For him "higher
Argument / Remains." The single thematic description of that
argument, presented with marvelous understatement, occurs
parenthetically in the midst of sarcastic comments on the substance of romantic epics. The speaker asserts as "Unsung" "the
better fortitude / Of Patience and Heroic Martyrdom." Mean-
while, both confidently and condescendingly, he derogates the
substance of earlier epics with their "fabl'd Knights / In Battles
feign'd," their "Races and Games, / Or tilting Furniture," their
"Impreses quaint" and "tinsel Trappings" and "gorgeous
Knights." There is more playfulness in this singing, I find, than
anywhere else in the prologues. It is born, perhaps, of a confidence the speaker now experiences. He is about to begin the
ending of his song, and he is completing the song of the prologues
within that larger epic song. Moreover, as he clearly indicates in
the final prologue, he has rediscovered his own fit role as singer.

As Christian singer, the poet-figure has made his choice of
subject. He has called for and received the illumination, raising,
and support he recognized in Prologues I and VII as requisite for
creative success. He has discarded his notions of singing in-
dependently of aid, and he has also abandoned his preoccupations
with his "personal" desires for renown and with his blindness. In
the progression of prologues, he has confronted to his own
satisfaction the interrelated subjects of self, song, and inspiration.
Now he argues a strong and lively case for his subject, and more
comfortably and surely than at any other point he declares his allegiance to and dependence on his muse,

> who deigns
> Her nightly visitation unimplor'd,
> And dictates to me slumb'ring, or inspires
> Easy my unpremeditated Verse.

The style he obtains from her is answerable to his "higher Argument." Argument and style will suffice to "raise / That name" "Heroic."

The final prologue begins with strength and harshness, as the speaker abruptly declares, "No more of talk where God or Angel Guest / With Man, as with his Friend, familiar us'd / To sit indulgent . . . I now must change / Those Notes to Tragic." He proceeds then to echo words and phrases from the opening prologues as he anticipates the substance of the imminent narrative: "disobedience," "a world of woe," and "Sin and her shadow Death." The sound, cadences, and conviction seem much the same as in Prologue I. And, though the speaker has now undergone much of the experience of his song and has, in that process, undergone changes in himself, his stance toward his muse and his poem also seems much the same as in Prologue I. Echoing that fine balance of confidence and humility in the poem's opening, the figure of the poet closes his own poem, the epic prologues, by willingly and wisely acknowledging his own frailty, while asserting the ultimately supreme role of the muse who governs always his song:

> higher Argument
> Remains, sufficient of itself to raise
> That name, unless an age too late or cold
> Climate, or Years damp my intended wing
> Deprest; and much they may, if all be mine,
> Not Hers who brings it nightly to my Ear.

The singer, losing himself in his singing, can now conclude that other "advent'rous Song."

"the hidden soul of harmony"

Milton's Knowledge of Music: Some Speculations

MORTIMER H. FRANK

When Edward Phillips detailed Milton's purchases of Italian music books,[1] he gave invaluable information. By noting that those books included works by Orazio Vecchi, Luca Marenzio, Don Carlo Gesualdo, Antonio Cifra, and Claudio Monteverdi, Phillips documented Milton's interest in a wide range of composers, some of whom created the finest and most avant-garde music of the time. And this documentation helps to explain Milton's praise of Lawes in his sonnet to the composer, indicates Milton's musical sophistication, and serves as a reminder that some of the references to music in Milton's writing cannot be understood fully unless they are read in the context of seventeenth-century music and the extraordinary stylistic changes affecting that music.

Achieving a clear understanding of Milton's musical references depends upon seeing such seemingly everyday musical terms as *harmony, fugue, chromatic,* and *symphony* in their seventeenth-century context. To the musician of the earlier seventeenth century, for example, "fugue" was simply polyphony, a polyphony greatly removed from the more intricately structured fugues of Bach and his contemporaries. Similarly, a seventeenth-century "symphony" was but a brief instrumental piece, as dif-

1. See James Holly Hanford and James G. Taaffe, *A Milton Handbook,* 5th ed. (New York, 1970), p. 336; also William Riley Parker, *Milton: A Biography* (Oxford, 1968), II, 830. According to Parker Cifra died "about 1638"; the correct date is 1629. References to Milton's poetry, unless otherwise noted, are to John Milton, *Complete Poems and Major Prose,* ed. Merritt Y. Hughes (New York, 1957).

ferent from the typical four-movement symphony of the late
eighteenth and nineteenth century as Thomas Nashe's *Un-
fortunate Traveller* is from James Joyce's *Ulysses*. To some, these
distinctions may seem obvious, but to others, whose musical
world is bounded by eighteenth- and nineteenth-century musical
traditions, such distinctions may not be clear. For example, James
Holly Hanford's comment on *Lycidas* ("No symphony was ever
composed of more varied emotional elements or blended them
more skillfully into artistic unity"[2]) might mislead an unwary
reader into thinking that the structure of *Lycidas* was similar to
that of a symphony by Beethoven or Brahms.

Clearly, Milton's musical sensibilities were shaped by a
tradition quite different from ours, and knowledge of *his* tradition
is necessary for an understanding of his musical references. The
most obvious case in point is his sonnet to Henry Lawes. As a
seemingly firm statement of admiration for Lawes's skill in fusing
music with words and in creating "tuneful and well measur'd
Song," this sonnet raises some significant questions: Should
Milton's opinion be taken literally? Did Milton hear in Lawes's
music, which today is valued less highly than that of many of his
contemporaries, a model of excellence? And, if so, was Milton's
own musical perspective consequently limited? Answering these
questions requires reading the sonnet in two contexts—that of the
conditions that occasioned it and that of the state of musical
evolution of the time.

The sonnet was originally titled "To my Friend Mr. *Henry
Lawes.*" The key word in that title is *friend*. Thirteen years
Milton's senior, Lawes was probably drawn to the Milton family
through a shared interest in music with the young poet's father;
and, as music master to the Earl of Bridgewater, he was probably
responsible for Milton's being engaged to write *A Mask,* better
known as *Comus.* What is more, Lawes had also been influential
in helping Milton avoid the complicated routine that usually
accompanied gaining permission to leave England when Milton
planned his continental trip in 1638.[3] With every reason to

2. Hanford and Taaffe, *Milton Handbook,* p. 139.

3. Lawes wrote Milton about having obtained for him "sufficient warrant to justify your
[Milton's] going out of the Kings Dominions." See *Complete Prose Works of John Milton,*
ed. Don M. Wolfe et al. (New Haven; 1953–), I, 339. Also see Nan C. Carpenter, "Milton
and Music: Henry Lawes, Dante, and Casella," *English Literary Renaissance* 2 (1972),
237–42.

consider Lawes a friend, Milton would have been strongly motivated to compose a poetic encomium to the composer. But that encomium is praising a musical practice as well, the practice of suitably wedding text to music, of making "English Music . . . span / Words with just note and accent." Failing to see these comments in their historical context is to be blind to Milton's musically progressive taste. And understanding why that taste was progressive requires understanding the musical traditions of Renaissance polyphony on which Milton was raised.

The traditions of that polyphony pervaded musical life in the Milton household: the elder Milton was himself an accomplished musician who contributed compositions to four of the more important vocal anthologies of his time.[4] It is reasonable to assume that the elder Milton's music was sung frequently in the Milton household and that the poet, with his keyboard ability and "delicate tuneable voice,"[5] was one of the performers. In performing that music the younger Milton surely learned the elements of Renaissance polyphonic style, the characteristic style of his father's music and a style that favored, above all, imaginative, quasi-independent melodies. To be sure, these melodies, when joined polyphonically, had to harmonize, but melodic rather than harmonic beauty was a composer's primary stylistic goal. And by striving for beautifully interlaced melodies, the composer had to sacrifice textual clarity, his text and its meaning often becoming blurred beyond comprehension. For example, in three- or four-part vocal polyphony in which each voice may be singing a different section of text, individual words become difficult to distinguish; consequently, the overall sense of those words may be particularly difficult to grasp. In addition, what Edmund H. Fellowes has called "complex cross rhythms between the parts"[6] often thicken the polyphonic web, contributing further to textual blurring.

4. Thomas Morley's *Triumphs of Oriana* (1601), William Leighton's *Teares or Lamentations* (1614), Thomas Myriell's *Tristitiae remedium* (1616), and Thomas Ravenscroft's *Whole Book of Psalmes* (1621). The elder Milton also composed music not included in these anthologies; see Ernest Brennecke, Jr., *John Milton the Elder and His Music* (New York; 1938), p. 153.

5. According to John Aubrey, Milton had "a delicate tuneable voice" and "good skill." "His father instructed him. He [Milton the poet] had an organ in the howse; he played on that most" (Oliver Lawson Dick, ed., *Aubrey's Brief Lives* [Ann Arbor, 1957] p. 202).

6. *The English Madrigal Composers* (Oxford, 1921), p. 124.

Even in purely instrumental Renaissance music, melody (rather than harmony) was a primary consideration, and artistic musical goals were reached, as in vocal polyphony, through fusing independent melodies; harmony, consequently, was more of a coincidental than a primary end.

For Milton this Renaissance polyphonic style exemplified a tradition that was as much in decline at the end of the sixteenth century as classical harmony was at the end of the nineteenth. That Milton turned with interest to contemporary trends is indicated by his purchases of music in Italy.

On the surface, the five composers identified in those purchases would seem to comprise an odd mixture. Monteverdi (1567–1643) was the only one alive when Milton went to Italy, and his contributions to western music are as significant and glorious as Milton's contributions to western literature. Called by one critic "the Aeschylus of music,"[7] Monteverdi composed in virtually every style of the late Renaissance and early baroque. His theatrical works were as catalytic to the growth of opera as Haydn's early orchestral works were to the growth of the symphony. In short, he was one of music's creative giants, whose range, imagination, and craftsmanship were unmatched, not only by his contemporaries, but by his immediate predecessors and followers as well.

Marenzio (1553–99), Vecchi (1550–1605), and Gesualdo (1560–1614) were all madrigalists, but they differed strikingly. "The first modern composer in the fullest sense of the word,"[8] Marenzio had a style "impossible to discover since for the special problems of every madrigal he sought special solutions."[9] In contrast, Gesualdo's style is consistently marked by chromaticism; indeed, his chromaticism is extreme to the point that his madrigals sound modern, even when measured against the standards of twentieth-century atonality. Vecchi, who displayed an "unsurpassed virtuosity in handling the choral medium,"[10] composed madrigal comedies in note-against-note style that, in contrast to Gesualdo's intense, somber chromaticism, are light and humorous.

7. Paul Henry Lang, *Music in Western Civilization* (New York, 1941), p. 339.
8. Ibid., p. 238.
9. Gustave Reese, *Music in the Renaissance* (New York, 1954), p. 420.
10. Lang, *Music in Western Civilization*, p. 238.

Cifra (1584–1629) may have been the least gifted of the five composers, but he was a fine craftsman who produced sacred music in the older polyphonic, contrapuntal style and secular songs with *ostinato* basses in the newer homophonic and harmonic idiom. Henry Lawes showed interest in these songs, and one writer has speculated that Lawes asked Milton to purchase them.[11]

This raises the question of whether or not Milton's purchases of music in Italy, diversified as they were, provide any clue to his own taste and preferences. Did he, for example, buy some things for his father and others for himself? Or did Lawes possibly suggest some of the composers to him? About the latter question one may never be certain, but it seems unlikely that Milton's father, who in 1638 was a musical conservative,[12] would have been interested in any of these composers, for despite their apparent diversity they share, apart from the general excellence of their work, one strikingly common trait: each composed vocal music in the new homophonic, harmonic style that (at the time Milton journeyed to Italy) had been flourishing in Italy for many years but was only beginning to evolve in England.

The state of English music at that period is well summed up by Ernest Brennecke, Jr., in his biography of Milton's father:

With the disappearance of the great composers of the elder Milton's prime, both the technique and the ideals which they had cultivated had given way to newer, more experimental, and quite revolutionary developments. In more senses than one the older system had achieved its heights and had died, and the succeeding system was still groping for that clear expression which it was not destined to achieve until the times of Purcell and of Handel. The ecclesiastical modes were dead; but modern harmony, based on the major and minor scales and keys, had not yet definitely arrived.[13]

But in Italy it had, and this new style, an outgrowth of the Italian desire for preserving textual clarity in vocal music, evidently appealed to Milton before he travelled to Italy. His purchases there suggest—in addition to his taste for music of varied emotional content and the interest an artist naturally has in

11. See the article on Cifra in George Grove, *Dictionary of Music and Musicians,* 5th ed. (New York, 1954).

12. See Brennecke, *John Milton the Elder*, p. 64.

13. Ibid., p. 116.

successful aesthetic innovation—the preference he implicitly expressed prior to his trip when he asked in *Ad Patrem* "what will support the melody of a pretty voice, / empty of words and sense, and of expressive rhythm?"[14] Italy offered Milton the best of the new vocal music, a chance to hear and buy the works of composers who, unlike their English counterparts, had brought to one stage of fruition some of the most radical stylistic changes in the history of western music.

What caused these changes? Chiefly the advent of opera at the close of the sixteenth century. In part, opera had sprung from "a desire to find a new musical vocal style for the humanistically inclined singer,"[15] the singer who was concerned with the preservation of texual clarity in musical settings of poetry. The effects of these changes were enormous. As one music historian has put it:

> The emergence of the *stile rappresentativo* or recitative about the year 1600 has often been regarded as the most important turning point in the entire history of music. The deliberate renunciation of polyphonic style set an end to the renaissance and brought to the fore a new principle: the solo melody with a chordally conceived accompaniment.[16]

The *stile rappresentativo* gave rise to two harmonically oriented vocal styles: one was recitative having "a static bass that amounted to series of pedal points"; the other, "a song-like melody with a more vivid bass line."[17] In essence, what emerged from the *stile rappresentativo* was a musical structure conceived not polyphonically or horizontally upon interwoven melodies, but homophonically, vertically, and by extension harmonically, with music being the servant of a sung text.

The shift in musical style that sprang from this concern for preserving texual clarity created a parallel shift in musical theory. As early as 1581 Vincenzo Galilei, father of the astronomer and a member of the Camerata (the Florentine literary and artistic

14. From the translation of the Latin (ll. 50–51) printed in *The Complete Poetry of John Milton,* ed. John T. Shawcross (New York, 1971), p. 168. For discussion about the date of the poem (most likely 1631–32) see *A Variorum Commentary on the Poems of John Milton,* ed. Merritt Y. Hughes, (New York, 1970), I, 232–40.

15. Lang, *Music in Western Civilization,* p. 235.

16. Manfred F. Bukofzer, *Music in the Baroque Era* (New York, 1947), p. 25.

17. Ibid., p. 29.

society credited with fathering the recitative style), wrote *Dialogo della musica antica e della moderna* in which he renounced the older polyphonic style in favor of a more homphonic, harmonic structure.[18] In 1602 Giulio Caccini, in the preface to his *Nuove Musiche,* condemned the "old" music for "not suffering the words to be understood by the hearers."[19] And about 1615 in England, Thomas Campion, in *A New Way of Making Fowre Parts in Counter-point,* called the bass—the voice on which harmony in the modern sense is most dependent—"the foundation of the whole song."[20] This view contrasts sharply with Renaissance theory and practice, which considered the next-to-the-lowest voice, or occasionally the middle voice, the foundation of a work.

In addition to causing the bass to gain prime significance, recitative and opera, with their interdependence of music and language, encouraged the association of music with one of language's most significant disciplines—rhetoric. This association strengthened the belief in the "affective" and persuasive powers of music. Not surprisingly, then, Henry Peacham, whose writings reveal a broad knowledge of the music of his time,[21] could state in 1622 in his *Compleat Gentleman:*

> Yea, in my opinion no rhetoric more persuadeth or hath greater power over the mind [than music]; nay, hath not music her figures, the same which rhetoric? What is revert but her antistrophe? her reports, but sweet anaphoras? her counterchange of points, but antimetaboles? her passionate airs but prosopopoeias?[22]

Viewed in this overall historical context, Milton's praise of Lawes's ability to teach "English Music how to span / Words with just note and accent" is more than an expression of admiration for a special talent: implicitly it expresses Milton's delight in the musical changes wrought by the *stile rappresentativo,* a delight implied earlier in *Ad Patrem* and further suggested by the one stylistic trait common to all the composers

18. See Oliver Strunk, *Source Readings in Music History* (New York, 1950), pp. 302–22.

19. Ibid., p. 378.

20. *The Works of Thomas Campion,* ed. Walter R. Davis (New York; 1967), p. 327.

21. See Morrison Comegys Boyd, *Elizabethan Music and Musical Criticism,* 2nd ed. (Philadelphia, 1974), pp. 83, 117, 136–37, 213–16, 218, 224.

22. See Strunk, *Source Readings,* p. 337.

whose music Milton purchased in Italy. In praising Lawes, Milton was welcoming the *stile rappresentativo* in England, recognizing, in effect, the passing of the older polyphony of his father and his father's contemporaries and the arrival of a new musical order, which was as different from the music of his father's time as Stravinsky's *Sacre du printemps* (1913) is from Brahms's *Fourth Symphony* (1885), works which, although seemingly a century apart, are separated by relatively few years.

As a poet, Milton probably was delighted with the new attention given to texts in musical settings, and as a musician with technical understanding of the stylistic changes occurring in music, he had to have had in mind an up-to-date implication of the musical terminology he used in his own verse. To be sure, when Milton writes of angels blowing "uplifted" trumpets,[23] he may have intended an allegorical abstraction, but when he speaks of the "Ceremony"[24] or "regal sound"[25] of trumpets, he most likely had in mind the music of his own time, possibly that of the very composer whose music he purchased in Italy. One has but to hear the opening orchestral toccata of Monteverdi's *Orfeo* (1607) with its regal, ceremonious trumpet fanfares to recognize the aptness of Milton's characterization of that instrument, which had become in Milton's time a prominent member of the opera orchestra. Moreover, this toccata, with its repetitions or "reports," its "reversions" or "antistrophes," its static reiteration of C-major, and its initial pronouncement of the note C by the bass viols, offers striking evidence of how up-to-date were the theories of Peacham and Campion and how far removed from the style of Renaissance polyphony was the style of Italian opera.

Certainly that operatic style has relevance to Milton's musical knowledge. The likelihood of his knowing Monteverdi's *Orfeo* has been suggested by Gretchen L. Finney,[26] who cites that opera as a source for *Lycidas*. If Finney is correct, her thesis supports Milton's knowing Monteverdi's music before going to Italy and offers another indication that his purchases of music there reflect a

23. "At a Solemn Music," l. 11.
24. *Paradise Lost* I.753.
25. *Paradise Lost* II.515.
26. *Musical Backgrounds for English Literature, 1580–1650* (New Brunswick, 1962), pp. 207–19.

previously acquired taste.[27] And James Holly Hanford has suggested that Milton, while in Italy, may have witnessed a performance of Monteverdi's *Arianna*.[28] Even if this is not so, the probability of Milton's having known the "Lament" from the opera is strong because that aria was one of Monteverdi's most admired pieces, so much admired, in fact, that composing an Arianna lament became a fashionable practice pursued by many composers, among them Milton's friend Henry Lawes.[29] Most significantly, Monteverdi's "Lamento d'Arianna" serves as a paradigm of the kind of music Milton was lauding in his sonnet to Lawes. And this similarity offers a possible explanation of why Milton used "English" in that sonnet. On the surface, the word might seem gratuitous; Milton's readers surely would have known that Lawes composed English music. But "English" implicitly distinguishes Lawes's works from those of some other national origin, a distinction that—in the context of operatic style flowering in Italy before it did in England—separates Lawes from any Italians who may have influenced him and, in so doing, suggests Milton's knowledge of the Italian aria style, which, like the style Milton praised in Lawes's music, is homophonic, chordal, and harmonic.

This harmonic structure of the new music of Milton's time is significant because it affects the meaning *harmony* would have had for him. Obviously he would have known the speculative, Platonic sense of the term, but Platonic harmony has nothing to do with harmony in the modern sense because "harmony [in that sense] did not exist in Greek music," which "was essentially melody and rhythm."[30] For Plato and other Greek theorists, *harmonia* defined a relationship between notes or *tonos* in a melodic scale,[31] a relationship different from the one created by notes simultaneously produced in a chord. Today chordal har-

---

27. "The date of the composition of *Lycidas* may be inferred from the cancellation in the Cambridge Manuscript, 'Novem: 1637' " (Hanford and Taaffe, *Milton Handbook,* pp. 134–35). This would place the poem's completion four months before the "probable" date when Milton went to the continent; see Parker, *Milton,* I, 169.

28. Hanford and Taaffe, *Milton Handbook,* p. 336.

29. Monteverdi's and Lawes's settings are compared by Pamela J. Willetts in *The Henry Lawes Manuscripts* (London, 1969), p. 8.

30. Curt Sachs, *Our Musical Heritage,* 2nd ed. (New York, 1955), p. 27.

31. Gustave Reese, *Music in the Middle Ages* (New York, 1940), p. 44.

mony, having pervaded musical life for the last three centuries, is taken for granted. But in Milton's time simple harmonic progressions (tonic-dominant-tonic, for example), were to him and his contemporaries—raised as they were in the modal musical traditions of Renaissance polyphony—fresh, exciting, and emotionally forceful. If one turns, for example, to symphonies from the early seventeenth-century masque, one discovers (in addition to the meaning of the term "symphony" in Milton's time) music of simple chordal and harmonic structure—music that for all its charm now seems rather commonplace. But to seventeenth-century ears it was innovative. To appreciate, therefore, the meaning and force of the term *harmony* for Milton, one must try to understand the emotional impact that harmonic music was making on the audiences of Milton's time. The word *try* is used advisedly, for what those audiences experienced emotionally can no more be recaptured today than can the shock generated by Beethoven's *Eroica* Symphony or Wagner's *Tristan* when they were first heard. For Milton, the term *harmony* was as progressive musically as the extraordinary departures from harmonic traditions in *Tristan* were to the audience at its premiere in 1865.

Milton's use of the term is often in keeping with its "modern" implications, its suggestion of the kind of union resulting when notes are united in a chord. He speaks, for example, of celestial voices "In full harmonic number join'd"[32] and of how a "harmony" can "hold all Heav'n and Earth in happier union."[33] When Milton writes of Adam and Eve and speaks of "Harmony to behold in wedded pair,"[34] the comment becomes an amplification of the "Union of Mind" mentioned in the preceding line. This is not to say that *harmony* did not have many overtones of meaning to Milton. But one of those meanings derives from the word's association in Milton's time with an innovative musical style of extraordinary impact, a style that made harmony more meta-phorically evocative than it can possibly be today.

That Milton was aware of the "modern" meaning of harmony is also suggested by other evidence. When Plato wrote "You cannot harmonize . . . that which disagrees"[35] he expressed a view

32. *Paradise Lost* IV.687.
33. "On the Morning of Christ's Nativity," ll. 107–8.
34. *Paradise Lost* VIII.605.
35. Benjamin Jowett, tr., *The Dialogues of Plato,* 4th ed. (Oxford, 1954), I, 518.

contradicted by seventeenth-century musical practices, practices that Henry Peacham recognized in asking: "How doth music amaze us when of sound discords she maketh the sweetest harmony?"[36] Anyone familiar with the music of the period (as Peacham was), will recognize in his question a literalness far removed from a clever use of paradox. What is more, a significant alteration made by Milton in "At a Solemn Music" indicates his own apparent familiarity with the kind of music Peacham had in mind when raising his question. The alteration, a replacement of three lines with five new ones,[37] bears on Milton's musical knowledge in that it involves the deletion of the word "chromatick." Milton's discarding of the word implies it had for him a meaning incongruent with the theme he wished to express, a meaning that probably was rooted in his own familiarity with the "modern" music of his time.

Chromaticism in the modern sense emerged in Italy during the late sixteenth century and exists in the madrigals of two of the composers whose music Milton purchased there, Marenzio and (as already noted) Gesualdo. Influenced by Italian models, a few English composers, most notably Thomas Weelkes (c. 1575–1623) and John Dowland (1563–1626), produced chromatic music during the first two decades of the seventeenth century. Milton therefore had opportunity to hear such music well before he wrote "At a Solemn Music" and before he journeyed to Italy. Even his father's stylistically conservative compositions contain a few occasional experiments with chromaticism.[38] In addition to knowing his father's music, Milton probably heard the popular music of Dowland,[39] who lived for a while near the Milton family and was likely to have been drawn to the musical activities in the Milton household.[40] Quite possibly the young poet witnessed Dowland performing on the lute his own hauntingly chromatic fantasies.

36. See Strunk, *Source Readings*, p. 337.
37. The three deleted lines read: "by leaving out those harsh chromatick jarres / of sin that all our musick marres / & in our lives & in our song." *The Works of John Milton*, ed. Frank Allen Patterson, et al. (New York, 1931–38), I,ii, 424. In Milton's revision, lines 19–25 replace the deletion.
38. See Brennecke, *John Milton the Elder*, p. 78.
39. On Dowland's popularity see Diana Poulton, *John Dowland: His Life and His Works* (Berkeley, 1972), pp. 66–67.
40. See Brennecke, *John Milton the Elder*, p. 63.

Most important, by 1637, the year "At a Solemn Music" was completed and the year before he went to Italy, Milton must have understood that chromaticism, rather than being exclusively dissonant, was capable of producing—to use Peacham's words— "the sweetest harmony." Viewed in this context, Milton's deletion of "chromatick" from "At a Solemn Music" was obligatory, not because the music described in the poem may have been of the old polyphonic vocal style in which chromaticism was unlikely to occur,[41] but because "chromatick," with its strong suggestion of harmony, proved inappropriate as a modifier of "jarres of sin that all our music marres" and weakened the contrast Milton draws between earthly "harsh din" in music of "disproportion'd sin" on the one hand and "divine sounds" of "Sphereborn," "harmonious" "Hymns" on the other.

Acknowledging this rationale in Milton's mind sheds no new light on the poem, but it does illuminate its author. For one thing, it offers still another indication that his purchases of music in Italy were the outgrowth of a cultivated, previously acquired taste for the avant-garde; more specifically, his interest in Marenzio and Gesualdo was not simply the reflection of his curiosity about two talented composers but the expression of a musical taste that, by 1638, had been formed in part by an appreciation of the chromatic style. What is more, Milton's use and subsequent deletion of "chromatick" supply additional evidence of how his musical allusions were not confined to speculative music.

Recognizing this lack of confinement is vital to understanding some of the references Milton makes to musical modes, references that often have been assumed to derive from ancient classical sources. In some of these references an ancient context may be appropriate,[42] but in others an early seventeenth-century implication may exist, an implication that modern readers cannot grasp without distinguishing between the ancient Greek modes and the modes of later periods.

The need for this distinction results from tenth-century monks' having confused church modes with the modes of ancient Greece. As a consequence of this confusion the church modes acquired names identical to those of their ancient counterparts.[43] But

41. Ibid., p. 118.
42. E.g., *Paradise Regained* IV.257.
43. See Sachs, *Musical Heritage*, pp. 29–33.

counterpart, in the final analysis, is hardly the appropriate word, for by the middle of the sixteenth century, with Greek names still in use (Lydian, Dorian, Phrygian, etc.), the musical modes had no more resemblance to the Greek modes than the "symphonies" of Henry or William Lawes, say, have to the symphonies of Gustav Mahler. Although Plato, for example, ascribed to each of the modes an ethical trait,[44] ascriptions with which Milton was surely familiar, those ascriptions may not always have relevance to Milton's references to the modes in his own verse. Fifty years ago, Merritt Y. Hughes recognized this when, in discussing the significance of "Lydian melody" in *L'Allegro,* he saw in Milton "the protest of a mind aesthetically mature against the moralistic and reactionary elements in the Platonic tradition."[45]

As in that tradition, each of the musical modes in common use in Milton's time was associated with particular "affects" or ethical qualities. But these qualities were in no way related to those set down by Plato. Plato's Lydian mode, for example, is "intimate and lascivious,"[46] whereas the Renaissance Lydian is *"vernaculis cantilenis & saltationibus aptus"* (apt for vernacular songs and dances).[47] It is reasonable to assume that Milton, with his wide-ranging intellectual curiosity and highly cultivated musical sensibility, would have had a knowledge of late sixteenth- and early seventeenth-century theories, a knowledge that would have enabled him to distinguish those theories from Platonic theory. And this assumption is strengthened by some of the references to the modes in his verse.

Before looking at the verse, however, it is well to demonstrate how practical and removed from abstraction ethical ascriptions to music may be, for a modern listener may question whether a mode (or, to use modern terminology, a key) can really be "lascivious" or "apt for vernacular songs." An answer to such a question may be had by thinking of ethical musical practices closer to today's culture. For example, G-minor is often called Mozart's "tragic" key; E-flat major, Beethoven's "heroic" key. Even more to the

44. On Plato's ethical theories of music see Reese, *Music in the Middle Ages,* pp. 44–45.

45. "Lydian Airs," *Modern Language Notes* 40 (1925), 137.

46. Reese, *Music in the Middle Ages,* p. 44.

47. See D. P. Walker, "Musical Humanism in the 16th and Early 17th Centuries," *The Music Review* 2 (1942), 224. The Lydian mode had a "tonic" of F and may be represented as a white-key piano scale beginning on that note; this mode was occasionally called Mixolydian.

point, perhaps, is the common modern association of a "major" key (or mode) with joy and extroversion; a "minor" key (or mode) with melancholy and introversion. How many military marches, after all, are composed in a "minor" mode? How many funeral marches in a "major" mode? Viewed in this context, the ascription of ethical qualities to a particular mode does not appear as theoretical and abstract as it otherwise might.

Still one more issue deserves consideration before examining some of Milton's references to the modes. As already noted, the conventions of Renaissance modal polyphony were decaying quickly in Milton's time. One may wonder, therefore, to what extent the Renaissance ethical views of music became part of this decay. Three theorists, whose views span a century, provide an answer. The first of them, Marin Mersenne (1588–1648), a priest and mathematician, wrote several important theoretical books on music. His characterization of the modes, published in 1623, is important because it synthesizes accumulated Renaissance tradition. It was Mersenne who called the Lydian mode "apt for vernacular songs and dances." Speaking of the Ionian mode, he said it is *"bellicosus"* (warlike).[48] The Ionian mode may be represented as a white-key piano scale beginning on the note C, in short, the key of C-major. Writing seventy years after Mersenne, the French composer Marc Antoine Charpentier (1634–1704) called C-major "gay and warlike,"[49] and in 1721, twenty-eight years later, Johann Mattheson (1681–1764), the most important German theorist of his time, called C-major *"rude und freche"* (rude and arrogant).[50] Although these attributed "affects" vary somewhat from one theorist to another, there is more than a thin thread of similarity that binds them, a similarity implying that the Renaissance ethical theories of music maintained a tenacious hold on musical life long after the collapse of Rennaissance musical style. And the significance of this implication bears directly on a few passages in Milton's verse.

One of them occurs in *L'Allegro*. The request of the poem's persona, "Lap me in soft Lydian Airs" (136), becomes more than

48. Walker, "Musical Humanism," p. 223. The Ionian mode was occasionally called Dorian.

49. See Don L. Smithers, *The Music and History of the Baroque Trumpet Before 1721* (Syracuse, N.Y., 1973), p. 237.

50. *Das neu-eröffnette Orchester* (Hamburg, 1721), p. 240.

merely a vague or exclusively Platonic allusion when one thinks of Mersenne's characterization of the Lydian mode as "suitable for vernacular songs and dances." The appropriateness to *L'Allegro* of this characterization may be recognized when one remembers that the poem is a companion to *Il Penseroso* and that each poem complements the other. As Hanford notes:

> Studies of the poems' progressive emphasis upon sound, music, and light have revealed their complementary natures and indicated the way in which the "pealing organ" and "full voic'd choir" of *Il Penseroso* culminate a movement begun in *L'Allegro*. The sensual music of that "Lydian air" is made explicitly Christian in the concluding lines of *Il Penseroso* and the speaker's merger of the two worlds—pagan and Christian—is figured in the images of sound of the two poems.[51]

But Mersenne's use of the term "vernacular," a word that for him, a Roman Catholic priest, probably would have implied the secular rather than the sacred, makes his ascription to Lydian as appropriate to the overall complementary context of "Lydian Airs" in *L'Allegro* as the Platonic sense of "sensual" is. This in no way precludes Milton's having had the Platonic sense in mind. But it offers the possibility that Platonic tradition was not the exclusive source of his implied meaning and not exclusively responsible for shaping his ideas about musical ethos.

And this possibility is suggested further by a passage in *Paradise Lost* in which the assembled fallen angels "move / In perfect *Phalanx* to the *Dorian* mood / Of Flutes and soft Recorders."[52] Mersenne calls the Dorian mode *"tibijs . . . maxime vero rebus diuinus atque religiosis amicus est"* (suited for flutes . . . but most appropriate for divine and religious things).[53] Milton's use of "flutes" and "recorders" is obviously in keeping with Mersenne's views; indeed, if Milton had some knowledge of Mersenne or of other theorists whose ideas Mersenne echoed, then this passage from *Paradise Lost* carries additional meaning, since Mersenne's comments, with their reference to religion and divinity, amplify (in the context of the fallen angels) the irony that characterizes much of the action in Hell.

51. Hanford and Taaffe, *Milton Handbook,* p. 121.
52. I.549–51.
53. See Walker, "Musical Humanism," p. 224. The Dorian mode had a "tonic" of D and may be represented as a white-key piano scale beginning on that note; this mode was occasionally called Phrygian.

Milton's possible knowledge of seventeenth-century musical ethos throws light on the conclusion of *Lycidas*. Milton's use of "Doric" to describe the "lay" "warbled" by the "uncouth Swain" has been taken to mean rustic. In the context of the tradition of the pastoral elegy that shaped *Lycidas,* such meaning was surely intended. But another meaning may have also been implied, one growing out of Mersenne' claim for the Dorian mode's suitability for "divine and religious things." In her argument for Monteverdi's *Orfeo* as a source of *Lycidas,* Gretchen L. Finney cites the opera's concluding *sinfonia* in the Dorian mode as a parallel to the "Doric lay" at the conclusion of the poem.[54] The opera's conclusion alters the traditional myth by having Orfeo (instead of being torn apart by Thracian women) asend to "heaven," gaining, like Lycidas, immortality.[55] Monteverdi's choice of the Dorian mode for the *sinfonia* that follows that ascension underscores, in the context of Mersenne's ascriptions, the Christian theme of the opera's conclusion. Similarly, Milton may have intended "Dorick" to suggest a Christian idea of divinity, a suggestion that would be in keeping with Christian allusions made earlier in the poem[56] and with the immortality gained by Lycidas himself.

Keeping in mind the importance of music in Milton's life enriches other passages in his writing. When he recommends, for example, in his essay *Of Education* the study of "the solemn and divine harmonies of music," one can recognize the recommendation of a musician who has experienced firsthand the worth of such study. And in *Areopagitica,* when Milton, with seeming hyperbolic irony, calls for "licensing" dancers and for "licensers to examine the lutes, the violins, and the ghittars in every house," one realizes that for the trained musician, who could no more suffer censorship of music than could the experienced poet suffer censorship of literature, this comment—ironic though it remains—can hardly be viewed as hyperbole. But more important perhaps, Milton's knowledge and love of music serve as a reminder of the breadth of his humanism. Certainly, to move closer to the music of his time is to approach more closely the man himself.

54. Finney, *Musical Backgrounds,* p. 215. Plato's Dorian is "manly and strong" (Reese, *Music in the Middle Ages,* p. 44) and seems ill-suited to the context of "Dorick" in *Lycidas.*

55. This is the revised (1609) version; the first (1607) edition of the libretto ends with Orfeo being destroyed.

56. E.g., lines 109, 173, 181.

Milton's Revolution against Rime, and Some of Its Implications

J. MAX PATRICK

For over three decades, from 1937 to 1968, and then posthumously in 1971, William Riley Parker battled against the "traditional" assumption that *Samson Agonistes* was composed in 1667–69 and was Milton's last poetic creation.[1] This assumption was evoked by the fact that it was published in Milton's old age and seemed an appropriate swan song for a blind poet in political defeat.[2] Parker argues so persuasively against this late dating and in favor of his "conjecture . . . of 1647 as the time when Milton wrote a moving drama on man's great temptation to withdraw"[3] that Oxford University Press allowed him in *Milton: A Biography* (1968) to assign the tragedy to 1647, that is, to place it thirteen years after *Comus* and two decades before the publication of *Paradise Lost*. "I have put it," asserted Parker, "where any responsible biographer would—in the place where, in my total picture of Milton's intellectual and artistic development it would

---

1. "The Date of *Samson Agonistes*," a paper read to the Johns Hopkins Philological Association on March 18, 1937; an article with the same title, *Philological Quarterly* 28 (1949), 145–66; "The Date of *Samson Agonistes*: A Postscript," *Notes and Queries*, n.s. 5 (1958), 201–2; *John Milton: A Biography*, 2 vols. (Oxford, 1968), pp. 313–22, 332, 431–32, 614, 903–17, 936–37, et passim (henceforth cited as Parker, *Milton*); "The Date of *Samson Agonistes* Again," in *Calm of Mind: Tercentenary Essays on* Paradise Regained *and* Samson Agonistes *in Honor of John S. Diekhoff*, ed. Joseph Anthony Wittreich, Jr. (Cleveland, 1971), pp. 163–74.

2. See James Holly Hanford, "*Samson Agonistes* and Milton in Old Age," in *Studies in Shakespeare, Milton, and Donne* (New York, 1925), pp. 167–89; reprinted in Hanford's *John Milton: Poet and Humanist* (Cleveland, 1966), pp. 964–86.

3. Parker, *Milton*, p. 910.

99

seem most logically to belong."[4] Moreover, as a result of his arguments, at least two chronologically arranged modern editions of Milton's poetry printed *Samson* before both *Paradise Lost* and *Paradise Regained*.[5] Nevertheless, as far as I can judge, most Milton specialists remain unconvinced or only partially convinced by Parker or regard the composition dates as an open, unresolved problem. Allan H. Gilbert, noting that Dalila was slighted in the argument of *Samson Agonistes* and that its transitions were weak, decided that it belonged to an earlier date than Parker's and that Milton had intended to revise it later; A. S. P. Woodhouse assigned it to the early Restoration period because of what seemed to be references to it.[6]

In the essay that follows, I discredit Parker's early dating of *Samson Agonistes* in order to accomplish three positive purposes—(1) to demonstrate that extant documentary evidence points to 1665–67 as the time when Milton had dictated *Paradise Lost,* had not yet begun to dictate *Paradise Regained,* and was chiefly engaged in dictating *Samson Agonistes;* (2) to examine the causes, development, and significance of Milton's turning against rime in the 1660s and to contend that this revolutionary change was probably precipitated by his composing the intricate rimed portions of *Samson Agonistes;* and (3) to qualify both of the

4. Ibid., p. 906.

5. *The Complete English Poetry of John Milton,* ed. John T. Shawcross (New York, 1963, and Garden City, 1963). (In his revised Anchor edition [1971] Shawcross still assigned *Samson Agonistes* to "1646–48?; revised, 1653 or later," but he restored it to "standard placement" after *Paradise Regained.*) *The Poems of John Milton,* ed. John Carey and Alistair Fowler (London and New York, 1968).

6. Allan H. Gilbert, "Is *Samson Agonistes* Unfinished?" *Philological Quarterly* 28 (1949), 98–106; A. S. P. Woodhouse, "*Samson Agonistes* and Milton's Experience," *Transactions of the Royal Society of Canada,* 3rd ser., 43 (1949), 157–75. (Woodhouse's contention that *Samson* was written right after the Restoration was anticipated by William Hayley in 1796, Charles Dunster in 1809, and A. J. Church in 1872; see Parker, "The Date . . . Again," p. 169.) Ernest Sirluck attacked Parker's dating of *Samson* in "Some Recent Changes in the Chronology of Milton's Poems," *Journal of English and Germanic Philology* 60 (1961), 749–85. Ants Oras argued for the traditional dating in "Milton's Blank Verse and the Chronology of his Major Poems," in *SAMLA Studies in Milton,* ed. J. Max Patrick (Gainesville, 1953), pp. 128–97. In "The Chronology of Milton's Major Poems," *PMLA* 76 (1961), 345–58, John T. Shawcross countered Oras's case for late dating by using the same statistics to support Parker's case. Oras replied in *Blank Verse and Chronology in Milton,* University of Florida Monographs, Humanities, no. 20 (Gainesville, 1966), and J. Max Patrick challenged his contentions when he reviewed this monograph in *Seventeenth-Century News,* 25:2 (1967), item 3.

preceding theses by putting the dating problem into a larger perspective.

Milton's friend and former pupil Thomas Ellwood relates that when the poet was living in Chalfont St. Giles to avoid the plague—that is, about August, 1665—Milton gave him a manuscript which Ellwood identified as "that Excellent Poem, which he entituled *PARADISE LOST.*"[7] Moreover, Milton's nephew Edward Phillips told John Aubrey that *Paradise Lost* was written in four or five years,[8] and scholars are in general agreement that they were about 1658–65, more or less. It seems clear, accordingly, that Milton had composed his major epic by about August, 1665. (This does not rule out his making some revisions later.) Publication was delayed by the Great Fire of 1666. The license bears no date, but it must have been obtained before April 27, 1667, for the contract with the printer, Samuel Simmons, bears that date and refers to the license. And the entry in the Stationers' Register is dated August 20.[9] The first issue became available then or soon thereafter. Thus there was at least a two-year interval between the completion of the manuscript of *Paradise Lost* that Ellwood read, about August, 1665, and its publication, about August, 1667.

What, if anything, was Milton composing during those years?

The seemingly obvious answer is that when he finished his long epic on *Paradise Lost* he next turned to creating his short epic on *Paradise Regained.* This conjecture seems neatly reasonable because of the parallelism of the titles, the generic closeness of the two works, and the appropriateness of regarding the short epic as a sequel or companion of the longer one. Moreover, it could be argued that Milton conceived *L'Allegro* and *Il Penseroso* concurrently or in quick succession and probably did the same with the epics. However, a close interrelatedness between two works by the same author is not in itself proof that they were conceived as twins or brought forth in immediate sequence. Tennyson published *Locksley Hall* in 1842 and Samuel Butler published

7. This and all subsequent quotations from Ellwood are from *The History of the Life of Thomas Ellwood . . . Written by His Own Hand* (London, 1714), pp. 233–34.

8. Helen Darbishire, ed., *The Early Lives of Milton* (London, 1932), p. 13.

9. Parker, *Milton*, p. 1107, n. 26.

Erewhon in 1872, but neither of them envisaged the sequel he added years later. And when Milton wrote *Pro Populo Anglicano Defensio* he had no thought of following it three years later with a sequel or companion piece entitled *Defensio Secunda*. It is unsafe to assume that Milton moved directly from *Paradise Lost* to composing its companion; and there is no documentary evidence to support this conjecture.[10]

On the other hand, there is some evidence that Milton did not turn to *Paradise Regained* when, sometime before about August, 1665, he finished the manuscript of *Paradise Lost* that Ellwood read. According to Edward Phillips, "*Paradice regain'd* . . . doubtless was begun and finisht and Printed after the other was publisht, and that in a wonderful short space considering the sublimeness of it."[11] Inasmuch as the title page in the early editions of *Paradise Lost* bears the date 1667 and copies of it went on sale about August of that year, Phillips' statement appears to mean that *Paradise Regained* was begun after about August, 1667. If so, there was an interval of over two years between Milton's finishing the manuscript of *Paradise Lost* before Ellwood read it in August, 1665, and Milton's beginning *Paradise Regained* sometime after August, 1667, when *Paradise Lost* was published—an interval in which Milton was not dictating either epic. However, Phillips' testimony is of dubious value, for he also asserts that *Paradise Lost* was "publisht in the year 1666."[12] Obviously he was presenting unverified impressions and approximate dates rather than accurately remembered facts. Apparently his impressions were that *Paradise Lost* was published about 1666 (that is, before March 25, 1667, in New Style calendar dating), and that *Paradise Regained* was not begun until sometime after that publication. This could mean that the interval

10. In the first line of the first edition (1671) of *Paradise Regained* ("I who e're while the happy Garden sung") Milton himself may refer to an interval between his singing—composing?—the two epics. The term "e're while" suggests *erewhile* or *whilere* (a while before, some time ago, or formerly) and also *e'er while* (before a while back) or *erstwhile* (a while ere now, some while ago, or even a little while ago or not long since). Certainly "e're while" is distinguishable from alternatives that Milton could have chosen, such as "I who" *just now* or *last year* or *till now* "the happy Garden sung," and therefore it does not imply that Milton turned to composing *Paradise Regained* as soon as he finished *Paradise Lost*. More important, "e're while," in contrast to "now" in line 2, makes clear Milton's *intention* to have *Regained* regarded as a later work than *Lost*.

11. Darbishire, *Early Lives*, p. 75.

12. Ibid., p. 75.

during which Milton was not dictating either epic could have been as little as seven or eight months. But whether that interval was less than a year or was two years or more, the problem remains. What was Milton composing during that interval?

Fortunately there is more reliable evidence that there was an interval and that it was appreciable. According to Ellwood, he found a temporary residence for Milton at Chalfont St. Giles in June, 1665, and there, about August, Milton handed him *Paradise Lost* to read. After he had done so, Ellwood returned and remarked to the poet, "Thou hast said much here of *Paradise lost;* but what hast thou to say of *Paradise found?*" Thereupon, Ellwood relates, Milton "made me no Answer, but sate some time in a Muse," and years later, in London, "he shewed me his Second Poem, called *PARADISE REGAINED;* and in a pleasant Tone said to me, *This is owing to you; for you put it into my Head, by the Question you put to me at* Chalfont; *which before I had not thought of.*"[13] Thus Phillips' statement that Milton began *Paradise Regained* "after the other was publisht" dovetails with Ellwood's making it clear that when *Paradise Lost* was completed by Milton, he "had not thought of" *Paradise Regained* and therefore obviously was not composing it. He may have devoted his time in whole or part to prose works such as *Accidence Commenced Grammar* (1669), *The History of Britain* (1670), or *Artes Logicae* (1671). However, it is generally agreed that these were earlier compositions. So what the testimonies of Ellwood and Phillips point to is that from August, 1665, or earlier, to the publication of *Paradise Lost* in 1667, Milton may well have been dictating *Samson Agonistes.*

Parker, noting that *Samson Agonistes* contains rimes, claimed that Milton's denunciation of rime in late 1667 or early 1668 made it "incredible" that Milton would have been composing in rime during the years immediately preceding that denunciation.[14] But Parker overlooked an alternative explanation: perhaps it was the composing of the complex rimed passages in *Samson Agonistes* that led Milton to decide to cease riming.

Following classical precedent, Milton avoided rime in his Greek and Latin poems. However, aware of the success of Shakespeare

13. See n. 7 above.
14. Parker, *Milton,* p. 904.

and other tragedians in using English blank verse and also aware
of the ample precedent for riming in the vernacular which was set
by Dante, Tasso, Chaucer, and others, Milton, at least until he
was fifty, recognized the validity of both rimed and blank verse in
English and other modern languages. From his two psalm
paraphrases in 1624 to his sonnets of about 1653–58, he composed about fifty-six English and Italian poems in rime. The four
rimed pieces in *Arcades* may be added to them, and also about a
fourth of the lines in *Comus*. Otherwise, unless Parker is right in
his conjecture that *Samson Agonistes* is datable about 1647,
Milton used unrimed English verse before 1659 in the rest of
Comus, in his imitation of Horace's Fifth Ode, and in the few
translations from classical poetry that he made, chiefly to quote in
his prose works. How far he intended to use or avoid rime in the
early projected tragedies is unknown: he possibly envisaged
alternating passages of rimed and blank verse in them, as in
Comus. At any rate, it is clear that until about 1659 Milton's
preference was for rime in shorter English poems, although he
was willing to use blank verse for some brief works and
dominantly in *Comus*. Presumably he utilized it in the masque for
the sake of variety and because, in such a long work, "the jingling
sound of like endings" could have a "trivial" effect and because
having to rime made him feel "vexation, hindrance, and constraint to express many things otherwise, and for the most part
worse then else" he "would have exprest them."

The words just quoted were dictated by Milton in the autumn
or early winter of 1667, after *Paradise Lost* had appeared and had
elicited a reaction that led Simmons, the printer, to procure from
Milton a book-by-book synopsis of the epic "for the satisfaction of
many that have desired it . . . and withall a reason of that which
stumbled many others, why the Poem Rimes not."[15] This "reason"
was published in a preliminary paragraph entitled "The Verse" in
the fourth issue of the first edition of *Paradise Lost*, either very
early in 1668 or very late in 1667. It was continued in later issues
and in the second edition. As a public announcement of Milton's

15. "The Printer to the Reader," prefixed to the fourth and following issues of the first
edition of *Paradise Lost*, preceding the paragraph on "The Verse." I quote them from the
Scolar Press facsimile of John Milton, *Paradise Lost 1667* (Menston, England, 1968),
appendix.

changed attitude toward rime and blank verse, its prime purpose was to justify his having composed his epic in *"English* Heroic Verse without Rime"; but he went far beyond that and attacked rime as a barbarous invention inessential to good poems, whether long or short, dramatic or heroic; and he also condemned it as a troublesome, trivial, unmusical, constraining bondage.

This published statement marked a radical change in Milton's attitude. His use of blank verse for approximately three-quarters of the lines in *Comus* suggests that even in the 1630s he found unrimed lines more pliable in long works and, except for special purposes, preferable in them. But at that time he had been far from rejecting rime: he used it in the rest of *Comus,* employed it masterfully in *Lycidas,* and continued its use in well over a dozen sonnets, various psalm translations, and other short poems up to 1659. However, within a decade of that date he was denouncing it as a "troublesome and modern bondage of Riming." Why did he change his mind? More specifically, what experience provoked this new attitude? And was that experience cumulative over many years or sudden?

The riming in the last five sonnets (composed about 1653–58) can hardly have caused Milton to alter his opinions. The pattern *cdceed* in the sonnet to Lawrence, with "rise" (l. 9) unmatched until "unwise" (l. 14) may suggest that Milton felt some awkwardness in composing it. But the two poems to Cyriack Skinner are straightforward enough; and the riming in the tribute to his late departed saint admirably overcomes the challenge of repeating the "a" sound in the end-words of the octet and the "i" in the sestet. And the rimes in the Piedmont sonnet are patently excellent and functional in onomatopoeic effects. They cannot have been easily attained; but a poet of Milton's virtuosity surely felt more satisfaction than vexation in achieving their sonorous intricacy. Nevertheless, the Piedmont and espoused saint sonnets do reveal what was both a weakness and a strength—Milton's tendency to set himself tough challenges, challenges whose conquest demanded extreme versatility. But the rimes in these two sonnets were obviously no more difficult to achieve than those in *Lycidas.* So we must look into the years *after* these sonnets, from 1659 on, for an explanation of Milton's changed attitude.

When Milton gave up the idea of treating the Fall of man in a

tragedy and decided to couch it in an epic, he must have entertained the feasibility and desirability of composing *Paradise
Lost* entirely in rime, or in blank verse interspersed with rime.
However, the earliest-composed part of it that we can identify is
in blank verse,[16] and there is no extant evidence of his ever having
rimed any part of it other than incidentally. For it does contain
occasional rimes—about 160 out of 5,282 possibilities (about 320
lines out of 10,565 in the second edition). This suggests that when
Milton composed *Paradise Lost* he was not yet as intent on
avoiding rimes as he was later in *Paradise Regained,* in which even
occasional rimes are quite rare—about 12 out of 1,035
possibilities (about 24 lines out of 2,070 in all; however, there are
also 12 instances of a word's being repeated at line ends, for
example "woe" at the ends of lines 398 and 399 in Book I; and in
one of these instances [Book I, ll. 377, 378, and 379] "lost" is used
3 times as a line-end word). It would seem that Milton's attitude
toward rime soured in the interval between the composing of the
two epics; if so, he made his decision against rime in the very
period between the Augusts of 1665 and 1667 when, as I have
contended, he was dictating *Samson Agonistes.* Apparently it was
with the writing of the rimed portions of that play that he
definitely rejected rime. But this was the end of a long cumulative
development.

   Samson Agonistes consists of 1758 lines. Robert T. Beum
found that 112 of them rimed; but he did not include slant rimes
or those occurring at intervals of more than four lines.[17] But
Parker, counting everything that could be regarded as a rime,
decided that there are "about 150 lines with rime (including *three
completely rimed stanzas*)" (italics his).[18] If we accept Beum's
figures, 1 out of 15.7 lines rime; if Parker's, 1 out of 11.7. For
Paradise Lost the figure would be 1 out of about 33. Thus the
quantity of riming in *Samson* is not markedly significant. What *is*
important is the nature of that riming—its sophistication. It is so
sophisticated and so difficult to achieve that the experience of

   16. *Paradise Lost* IV. 32–41, quoted by Phillips; Darbishire, *Early Lives,* p. 73; cf.
Parker, *Milton,* p. 857, n. 34.
   17. "The Rhyme in *Samson Agonistes,*" *Texas Studies in Literature and Language* 4
(1962), 177–82.
   18. Parker, *Milton,* p. 904.

composing it could well have precipitated Milton's rejection of riming as a troublesome bondage.

He seems to have found in rime a challenge and an opportunity for virtuosity. He also became increasingly conscious of the need to overcome or avoid the perils involved in riming. He listed most of those perils in that paragraph entitled "The Verse": they are the sacrificing of intended sense and clear statement in order to achieve rimed endings; laming meter in order to fit in rimes; being constrained to express things otherwise than one would have phrased them; having to see that words that require emphasis are placed in the riming positions; having to avoid the jingle of like endings; and having to prevent them from sounding trivial.

From early in his writing career Milton was obviously trying to avoid these pitfalls. He resorted to various means, most of them intended to soften or distract from the rime, to negate or weaken it, to throw the impact elsewhere, to frustrate the expectation of dingdong parallelism. He distanced riming words from each other; he put them in lines that had different numbers of feet or stresses; he made the sentence rhythms and the sense run over the line ends; he frequently overwhelmed mere rime by making it part of assonance patterns woven throughout a passage regardless of the line endings. Sometimes he used slant rimes or partial rimes or eye rimes: such imperfect marriages are *more* and *sere, excuse* and *muse, appeared* and *heard.* All these features are noticeable in the early lines of *Lycidas* and detailed analyses of them have been published by F. T. Prince, Ants Oras, and Joseph A. Wittreich, Jr.[19] Paradoxically, what these features reveal is an effort to have rime while at the same time annihilating, weakening, dispersing, or frustrating it.

The fact is that Milton's best rimed poems, as early as *Lycidas,* show him including rime far less as a source of ornament and musical beauty than as something to be weakened, retreated from, or triumphed over. Rime is a bondage, hindrance, constraint, or vexation—neither an ornament nor a necessity. It is the over-coming, the triumph over constraint and over bondage and vex-

19. F. T. Prince, *The Italian Element in Milton's Verse* (Oxford, 1954), pp. 71–88; Ants Oras, "Milton's Early Rhyme Schemes and the Structure of *Lycidas,*" *Modern Philology* 52 (1954), 14–22; Joseph Anthony Wittreich, Jr., "Milton's 'Destin'd Urn,' The Art of *Lycidas,*" *PMLA* 84:1 (1969), 60–70.

ation that really matters. And it is that triumph which inevitably brought to him as a virtuoso artist a sense of conquest and power and satisfaction. I do not deny that he achieved some beauty and true musical delight and sense variously drawn out from one verse to another or that these were his proper aims. Indeed, by the time that he dictated his public pronouncement about the verse in *Paradise Lost* he had come to recognize that these ought to be his goals. But in the main they were achieved despite, not because of, the rime.

That paragraph on "The Verse" is a highly significant statement. It is an open acknowledgement by Milton that, during a long creative career extending from as early as 1624 to 1659 when he was fifty years old, he had made a tremendous mistake. Instead of expressing things as he really wanted, and instead of devoting his genius primarily to the achievement of apt numbers, true musical delight, fit quantity of syllables, and the sense variously drawn out from verse to verse, he had, for the sake of the jingling sound of like endings, been "carried away by custom" to sacrifice aptness, music, and true sense faithfully expressed. This much Milton admitted. Parker calls the paragraph on "The Verse" a manifesto, a public rejection of rime;[20] but it might better be called a public confession, an admission of fault and of something close to stupidity. We may admire the aging poet for having the courage to make it.

Milton also admits what he could have faced long before but apparently was slow to recognize overtly—that rime is "no necessary Adjunct or true Ornament of Poem or good Verse." Why then did he use it so long? Was it merely that he, like his predecessors, was "carried away by custom"?

No doubt precedent and custom had their influence. But Milton was a radical. He had thrown off the bondage of precedent and custom when he turned against government of the church by episcopacy, of the state by monarchy, and of marriage and divorce by canon law. Admittedly in all these he was a conservative radical, moving forward to new attitudes by looking backwards to earlier precedents and customs. But why was he so slow to do likewise in his attitude toward something as important as versifying is to a poet?

20. Parker, *Milton*, p. 904.

The reason has already been suggested: Milton's practice in *Lycidas*, in the rimed portions of *Comus*, and in sonnets such as the one to his late departed saint reveals that instead of using rime as a necessary adjunct of good verse or as a true ornament of poetry, Milton resorted to it as something to be overcome, distracted from, deemphasized, weakened, and maimed; as a vexation, hindrance, and constraint to be overcome; in a nutshell, as a challenge to virtuosity.

In this he was typically baroque. To this day we gaze with amazement on baroque sculpture whose creators transcended the vexation, hindrance, and constraint of hard marble and miraculously transformed it into the semblance of what it was not, making it look like lace or delicate garments or flowing water. An obvious example is the swirled cloth of Bernini's St. Longinus.[21] For such a sculptor the resistant marble was a challenge to be overcome, something to be transcended and transformed; and when he did transmute it into the fragility of lace or the swirling of silken robes or the seeming flexibility of a rippling fountain, he experienced that sense of triumph which is characteristic of baroque artists. The result was frequently a thing of beauty, a source of true artistic delight—a coronet of gracious achievement. But in those serpentine folds, in the deceptive delicacy of the lace there lurked the serpent of exhibitionism. The triumph was not one of pure art: it involved an egotistic display of virtuosity and power exploited to amaze and astound the beholders.

Milton was by no means alone in this craving for power-gratification, show-off ornament, extravagance, ostentation, and versatility. It is a feature of the baroque. Marvell and Herbert were acutely aware of the problem and of what became the standard means of solving it, of eating one's cake and having it too. For one may indulge in this virtuoso display by at once using and damning it—as Marvell does in "The Coronet" and George Herbert in his "Jordan" poems when he related how he "sought out quaint words and trim invention . . . Curling with metaphors a plain intention, / Decking the sense as if it were to sell."

But we need not go beyond Milton. He had an obsession for

21. Gian Lorenzo Bernini's colossal statue of St. Longinus is in one of the four niches facing the Baldacchino in St. Peter's, Rome.

setting himself extreme challenges, for writing "Things unat-
tempted yet in Prose or Rhyme." *Samson Agonistes* is itself an
example, with its remarkable fusion of Hebraism and Hellenism.
Milton clearly set out in it not only to rival and match or surpass
the Book of Job but also to out-Greek the Greeks in their own
kind of tragedy. Similarly in his sonnet to Sir Henry Vane, Milton
was characteristically not satisfied to write just a sonnet; for it is a
fusion of three genres—verse epistle, character, and sonnet. Indeed, nearly everything that Milton wrote was a special performance. I need only point to *Lycidas:* it consists of 193 lines;
but scholars have shown that it summarizes and interprets all the
themes in the volume of memorial verses to Edward King; it is a
resolution of Milton's own fears of premature death; it uses time
as a dimension, interrelates two world views, contains an in-
terplay of Arcadian and real; it has a thesis, antithesis, and
synthesis; it expresses the Orpheus myth fused with Christ; it
contains a death / birth pattern; it is rich in patterned water
symbolism, and also in flower symbolism; it is a reworking of
literary archetypes and has rich surface meaning as well; its rime
and assonance patterns are incredibly complex; and scholars keep
publishing further insights into the poem.[22] Obviously Milton is
an astounding and virtuoso poet: the point needs no proving.

As described by Heinrich Wölfflin,[23] the essence of the baroque
is that the baroque artist has a thorough mastery of traditions and
conventions, but instead of remaining within them he exploits
them with reversals, dislocations, and something like distor-
tions—and does all this with incredible virtuosity. Certainly
Milton's works fall within this definition—perhaps more so than
those of any other English writer except possibly Donne and, on a
smaller scale, Herbert and Marvell.

Milton set himself fantastic challenges to overcome in his
poetry, often with resulting musical beauty and reinforced
communication of ideas and feelings. Nevertheless, some of this

22. For the scholars and works summarized in this sentence, see the survey of criticism
on *Lycidas* by Douglas Bush, in *A Variorum Commentary on the Poems of John Milton,*
ed. A. S. P. Woodhouse and Douglas Bush (New York, 1972), II, ii, 565–636.

23. *Renaissance und Barock* (Munich, 1888) and *Kuntgeschichtliche Grundbegriffe*
(Munich, 1915), passim. (My brief statement of Wölfflin's viewpoint is, of course, an
oversimplification.)

virtuosity seems poetically pointless—bravura for its own sake, triumph for the mere sake of triumph. His almost insatiable desire to overcome self-imposed difficulties is best seen in the discoveries of James S. Whaler in *Counterpoint and Symbol* (Copenhagen, 1946). Reduced to extreme simplicity, part of what Whaler demonstrates is that if the pauses in *Paradise Lost* are noted, certain patterns emerge: 1 syllable, pause; 2 syllables, pause; 3, pause; 4, pause; then 5 and 6, and then, in reverse, 6-5-4-3-2-1; or the pattern may be 2-4-6-8-10-12 and then the reverse thereof. Sometimes these progressions correspond to the content; for example, rising with the good angels and upward flights or falling with bad characters and descents and the like. But many of these and other more complicated series that Whaler observes seem to be little more than pointless exercises. There was, perhaps, a little more point in Milton's making *hundredfold* the hundredth word in the Piedmont sonnet. And Milton seems to have approached the challenges of riming somewhat similarly—setting himself challenges and triumphing over them. One instance is his ability to dispense with rime even though using it, as he does in *Lycidas,* where some of the lines do not rime with others.

It probably was while composing the rimed portions of *Samson Agonistes* between the summers of 1665 and 1667 that Milton changed his mind about riming. One cannot say that he over-challenges himself in those passages, for he undoubtedly suc-ceeded in them; but their exigencies seem to have been so great that, once they were conquered, he realized that the effort in-volved was excessive.

For example, lines 1010–17 of *Samson Agonistes:*

> It is not vertue, wisdom, valor, wit,
> Strength, comeliness of shape, or amplest merit
> That woman's love can win or long inherit;
> But what it is, hard is to say,
> Harder to hit,
> (Which way soever men refer it)
> Much like thy riddle, *Samson,* in one day
> Or seven, though one should musing sit.

In a sense this virtuoso passage rimes *aa'a'ba(a')ba: wit, merit, inherit, say, hit, refer it, day, sit.* But when read, these rimes almost disappear. The first end-word, *wit,* is overwhelmed in the cumulative force of the list. And since the accent falls on the first syllable of *merit,* its last syllable hardly rimes at all with *wit.* The sentence rhythm sweeps over the end of the second line so as to slur that *it* sound all the more (especially so if the second line is read with more than five stresses). The sense of riming is further obscured by Milton's giving the fourth line only four feet, and the fifth only two. Moreover, *refer it* in the fifth line does not really rime with *merit* and *inherit.* And although *day* does rime with *say,* one is in a fifth foot and the other in a fourth. *Hit* rimes with *sit;* but they are distanced by having two lines between them and by their different foot positions. Furthermore, the assonance and consonance patterns are so pervasive that it is their sound more than that of the riming that one hears. It is evident that achieving this kind of assonance-crammed riming verse is a fantastic challenge. I have dealt with only one instance of it in *Samson Agonistes.* If anything, the virtuosity is more extreme in some of the other rimed passages, such as lines 1697–1707; but it is less notable in the final "sonnet"—lines 1745–58.

It is, accordingly, probable that the writing of these intricate passages led Milton to see that the effort involved in riming them was excessive and to recognize that instead of using rime for beauty, emphasis, ornament, and coherence, he was deferring to custom by including it, but at the same time was trying to negate and obscure it. What he achieved rimed but approached a virtuoso annihilation of rime. The result was triumphant and astounding but "no necessary Adjunct . . . of Poem or good Verse, in longer works especially." Moreover, the practice was dangerous, for it could distract both author and reader from the true ends of poetry—beauty and significant ideas.

I have shown that the available documentary evidence indicates that *Paradise Lost* was completed by August, 1665; that the dictation of *Paradise Regained* was probably not begun until August, 1667, or later; and that Milton could have dictated *Samson Agonistes* in the interval between the two epics. Part of the evidence that he did so is the strong likelihood that the very exercise of composing the rimed portions of *Samson* induced Milton to desist from riming thereafter. And *Paradise Regained* is evidence that he did desist; for although it is difficult to avoid some occasional like line endings in a lengthy poem—even in the *Aeneid* there is no lack of them—Milton kept them infrequent in *Paradise Regained,* which I contend is his last work. Moreover, if he had composed rimed poems in his late period, surely he would have included them when he reprinted his 1645 volume in 1673 and added to it several previously unpublished rimed poems (such as the sonnet "I did but prompt the age") that he had composed before 1658.

In contending that Milton probably dictated *Samson Agonistes* largely in 1665–67 and that his revolution against riming was probably precipitated by his composing its intricate rimed passages, I have depended on available evidence, as Parker did in his attempts to assign the play to an early date. But some qualifications and further considerations are necessary; for much of the documentary evidence is questionable, and Parker's mistake must be avoided: he was too willing to build bricks with scant straw—to draw firm conclusions and to present them as established facts even when all the pertinent extant evidence amounted to but a tiny fraction of what must have existed originally. Certainly the evidence relative to *Samson Agonistes* provided by Ellwood and Phillips is both too exiguous and too questionable to allow either Parker's or my own conclusions (as given above) to be regarded as authoritative or definitive. Phillips is notoriously unreliable in the other "facts" that he supplies. And although Ellwood identifies the manuscript Milton gave him to read at his leisure as "that Excellent Poem, which he entitled PARADISE LOST," we cannot be sure that he received and read all ten books of what became the first edition. Indeed, his question, "Thou hast said much here of *Paradise lost;* but what hast thou to say of *Paradise found?*" may indicate that what he read was limited to the Fall and did not include the parts of the epic that treat its complementary theme, "till one greater Man / Restore us."

Moreover it is important to remember Milton's blindness. Lacking sight, he must have composed most of his poetry in his head, revising it, polishing it, and memorizing it in something close to a final state before he dictated it. No doubt he later imposed some changes on what he dictated. But he did not have a tape recorder or its seventeenth-century equivalent, a secretary who was available at all times; so, of necessity, he must have worked out passages rather fully before he dictated them. The true composition time of *Samson Agonistes* was less when he dictated it than the period or periods in which he invented, developed, and refined it within his mind. When he did so cannot, of course, be definitively ascertained. But common sense and the extant data permit a probable solution.

Scholars generally agree that Milton was intermittently working toward what became *Paradise Lost* from about 1640, when he included some play outlines on the Fall in the Trinity Manuscript. However, his own words, "long choosing, and beginning late," in *Paradise Lost* IX.26, suggest that he probably did not settle on its main scheme until sometime in the 1650s or even later. The Trinity Manuscript also shows that as early as 1640 he was interested in writing plays on aspects of the lives of Samson and Christ. But there is no mention there of either the destruction of the Philistine temple or the temptation of Jesus in the desert. When he chose them and how soon or late he began to work out in his mind what became *Samson Agonistes* and *Paradise Regained* can only be conjectured. My own notion is that he intermittently planned them and probably experimentally dictated some passages for both of them in the 1650s and early 1660s, originally intending to couple them as *Samson Agonistes* and *Christus Agonistes* within a trilogy of complementary and interrelated works that included *Paradise Lost,* but changed his mind when Ellwood's question led him to what he "had not thought of before"—the idea of entitling the temptation poem "Paradise Regained." At any rate, Milton gave publication priority to *Paradise Lost,* and this suggests that he gave it a like compositional preference. On the other hand, he probably kept all three works in mind; so that when he completed *Paradise Lost*— whether it was by August, 1665, or some months later—he had worked out the frameworks and some of the contents of the other two poems and probably had dictated some of them. It is conceivable that he wrote some or all of the rimed portions of the Samson play before about 1659, the date after which he is not known to have written any other systematically rimed poetry. But that very fact combined with his public turning aginst rime later, in 1667, and the absence of all but occasional rime in *Paradise Regained* lead me to stick to my contention that Milton composed the rimed portions of *Samson*—and therefore, almost certainly, most of the unrimed context—sometime before the declaration against rime, and that it was the very experience of creating those intricately rimed passages that led to his change of attitude. Thus my conclusion is that *Samson* was planned and partly composed before Milton completed *Paradise Lost,* but that its final composition and dictation took place after he finished the epic and before the declaration against rime and also before the main dictation of *Paradise Regained.* Accordingly, though admitting that the evidence is inconclusive, I still maintain that *Samson* was Milton's penultimate major work.

But one final consideration remains. Most editors try to realize their authors' intentions. Like them we may ask what, regardless of composition dates, was the order in which Milton intended his three last major works to be read. Whether *Samson Agonistes* was composed in 1647, as Parker conjectures, or was Milton's penultimate poem, dictated after *Paradise Lost* was finished and before the end of 1667, as I maintain, or was his last major work, as has been traditionally assumed, the fact remains that he published *Paradise Lost* first and some years later coupled the other two in one volume with *Samson Agonistes* in the terminal position. This suggests that Milton's intention was to have them read in that order and to have *Samson* regarded as the last work in what we may view as a trilogy of interrelated masterpieces.

APPENDIX: A Caveat Against Parker

A full answer to Parker's case against late and for early dating of *Samson Agonistes* would require a treatise and a great deal of close reasoning and, unless new evidence turns up, would not settle the dating problem. My purpose here is merely to comment on some aspects of his case.

The year 1647 is a conjecture on Parker's part about where *Samson Agonistes* seems logically to fit. Moreover, his position is rather vague and wavering. On page 910 of the *Biography* he admits that 1647 is conjectural. On page 432 he opines that "perhaps a draft of the tragedy was completed before September, 1653." But on page 468 he is more cautious: "As the year 1655 drew to a close, Milton's study contained a clutter of unfinished or unpublished literary and scholarly projects," and among them "probably an incomplete tragedy on Samson." But unless some passage in the biography has eluded me, Parker nowhere indicates when, before 1670, this "completed" draft of an "incomplete tragedy" was revised and finished; nor does he discuss the extent of such changes other than speculating on page 614 that Milton possibly "insisted on some last minute revision." However, despite the scholarly caution shown here and in his posthumous article on "The Date of *Samson Agonistes* Again," Parker does assign *Samson* to 1647 in his biography and treats this placement as a fact. Clearly it is more than a conjecture with him: it is a matter of belief. And to persuade his readers to accept his belief, he is willing to mislead them with partial truths and ambiguities.

For example: Edward Phillips decided that the time when *Samson Agonistes* was composed "cannot certainly be concluded." Clearly he considered various possible times but felt unable to fix on one. So Parker had some grounds for declaring on pages 904–5 that Phillips did not "believe" *Samson Agonistes* was composed in 1667–69. But it would be equally true to assert that Phillips did not "believe" *Samson* was composed in 1647 or any other date proposed by Parker. Thus Parker's statement could give an unwary reader the false impression that Phillips rejected 1667–69 as a possible dating.

Parker also asserts, on page 904, that "after about 1734 (no earlier . . .) it was . . . assumed that Milton's *Samson* was his last poem." This inverse way of alleging that before about 1734 no one ever assumed that Samson was the last work by Milton is perhaps meant to hide the bald assurance of so wording it. It is true that Richardson's publishing the "assumption" in 1734 is the first extant evidence of anyone's making it explicitly. But first publication of an assumption is not in itself proof that no one ever made it previously, especially where surviving data are slight. Anyway, Richardson may have made it years earlier; and we do not *know* that he lacked authority for it: after all, he had interviewed Milton's daughter Deborah. Furthermore, Phillips must have entertained the assumption or possibility that *Samson* was written late when he stated that *Paradise Regained* was written in a remarkably short period of time after *Paradise Lost* was published and then added that the date of *Samson* could not be certainly concluded; he obviously did not feel able to deny the possibility that *Samson* was a late composition.

Parker also made Phillips' ignorance of the date one of the reasons for assigning the play to 1647 by arguing that it must have been composed when Phillips was not living with or visiting Milton.* But such an early dating involves assuming that Phillips neglected to ask his Uncle John, "What have you been composing since I last saw you?" and also assuming that he did not learn from him or some member of the household that a major work on Samson had been dictated. It seems incredible that the family and Milton conspired to keep such a masterpiece hidden from Phillips. Surely a work that was among Milton's papers from 1647 on would have come to Phillips' attention sufficiently for him to have stated with assurance that it was begun and at least partially written before the two epics. The fact that he could not decide for sure when the play was written indicates a conclusion opposite to Parker's—that it was indeed a late work.

* Parker, "The Date of *Samson Agonistes*," reprinted in Ralph E. Hone, *John Milton's Samson Agonistes* (San Francisco, 1966), pp. 233–35.

"Subject for Heroic Song"

The Renaissance Michael and the Son of God

STELLA P. REVARD

Driving onward upon his foes, "gloomy as Night," the Son of God becomes at the climactic moments of Book VI of *Paradise Lost* a supreme battle hero. It is a surprising transformation, not only because as soldier the Son is taking on a role new for him in *Paradise Lost,* but also because traditionally the soldier of God and the victor in the heavenly combat had been Michael, not the Son. Milton, alone among Renaissance poets, mounts the Son in a conqueror's chariot, arms him with ten thousand thunders, and makes him drive Satan out of Heaven.

In effecting this transformation, Milton is quite aware that he is breaking tradition. Few Renaissance poets had accorded the Son any part in the war.[1] Few, in fact, had even differentiated God the Son from God the Father, except to allude to the Son's distant incarnation and future victories over Satan on earth. Only in Valmarana's *Daemonomachiae* (1623) does the Son as *Verbum Dei* have a significant role, appearing at the final moments of the war to strengthen Michael and to effect Satan's defeat, but not displacing the archangel as hero in battle.[2] In designating Michael

1. In some Renaissance accounts (see, for example, Friedrich Taubmann, *Bellum Angelicum,* in *Epulum Musaeum* [Leipzig, 1597] or Thomas Heywood, *The Hierarchie of the blessed Angels* [London, 1935]), envy of the Son's future exaltation as man motivates Lucifer's rebellion.

2. Odoricus Valmarana, *Daemonomachiae: Sive, de Bello Intelligentiarum Super Divini Verbi. Incarnatione, Libri XXV* (*sine loco,* 1623). Without the Son, says Valmarana, Michael could not have conquered the rebels: "Hoc sine nec Michael poterat vicisse rebelles" (Bk. I, p. 27).

as victor, Milton's predecessors follow Scripture quite literally:
the twelfth chapter of Revelation (verses 7–9) recounted that the
dragon and his angels did not prevail over Michael and his
angels.[3] The poets have not followed the line of some theological
commentary, which identified Michael with the Son (biblical
exegetes had argued that since Michael in Hebrew signifies "he
who is like God," the writer of Revelation might have meant to
designate Christ by that name). Neither do the poets deal with the
theological view that the war in Heaven described in Revelation is
not the war of Satan's original rebellion, but the war of Christians
on earth against Satanic evil. In his theological commentary, *De
Doctrina Christiana,* Milton is silent on the second point, that is,
which war of Satan is being described in Revelation 12, but he
does affirm that the Michael referred to in verses 7–9 is the archangel, not the Son. He argues, moreover, that the phrase *did
not prevail* indicates that Michael's forces did not win, but were
held at stalemate.[4] In *Paradise Lost* Milton carries this independent interpretation even further: he denies victory to
Michael and advances the Son in his place. Yet as the Son becomes
soldier of God, borrowing, as it were, Michael's armor and
equipage, many of the characteristics previously attributed to the
warlike archangel now accrue to the Son, as he, not Michael,
tramples Satan and returns triumphant to the Father. To un-

---

3. See, for example, Thomas Heywood, *The Hierarchie of the blessed Angells* (London, 1635). Heywood sets the verses from Revelation 12: 7–9 into couplets:

> Thus *Iohn* writes of the Battell: *Michael
> Fought, and his Angels, with the* Dragon *fel:
> The* Dragon *and His Angels likewise fought,
> But in the Conflict they preuailed nought . . .*
> (p. 340)

4. Among the seventeenth-century theological commentaries on Revelation, see David
Pareus, *In Divinam Apocalysim S. Apostoli et Evangelistae Johannis Commentarius*
(Heidelberg, 1618), p. 561. Pareus sums up an early tradition going back to Ambrose. See
also the marginal commentary in the Geneva Bible ("Revelation," *The Bible* [London:
Robert Barker, 1599], p. 115). This matter is discussed more fully in my article, "The Warring Saints and the Dragon: A Commentary upon Revelation 12:7–9 and Milton's War in
Heaven" *Philological Quarterly,* 53 (Spring 1974), 181–83. In *Christian Doctrine* (I, ix),
Milton describes Michael as "leader of the angels and 'Αντίπαλος (antagonist) of the prince
of the devils; their respective forces were drawn up in battle array and separated after a
fairly even fight, Rev. xii. 7, 8" (*Complete Prose Works of John Milton,* ed. Don M. Wolfe
et al. [New Haven, 1953———], VI, 347). For the original Latin see *The Works of John
Milton,* ed. Frank Allen Patterson et al. (New York, 1931–38), XV, 104.

derstand the new role the Son assumes, one must look first at the Renaissance Michael.

The Michael who, in the Renaissance epics and dramas, not only wages but wins the war is a far more important character than the Michael of Book VI of *Paradise Lost*. Primarily a warlike angel, the greatest of soldiers, he is more than just a military leader. This angel, splendid in appearance and lit by zeal for God's cause, is Lucifer's opposite, a fitting foil to the "morning star," by tradition highest and most beautiful of the angels. He is a spokesman for God, and his loyalty contrasts with Lucifer's perfidy. The victory he wins over Lucifer and his rebels is a victory of faith as well as military force. It is not surprising then that the Renaissance Michael influenced Milton in the depiction of his own warring archangel and his hero Son.[5]

Most prominent in the Renaissance Michael is the charisma of a leader. As the Italian poet Murtola and the Spanish Acevedo describe him in their Creation poems, he shines in arms. Murtola tells of his freshness and youth, his blond hair and rosy complexion, and Acevedo of the resplendent gold and diamond of his armor.[6] In Taubmann's *Bellum Angelicum* (1597), there is a detailed portrait of the well-armed angel with shining breastplate, scaly bronze armor, and jeweled sword.[7] The sword figures

5. In this essay I have not attempted to prove Milton's debt to specific poets but only his general debt to a tradition wherein Michael appears as the hero of the war in Heaven. Those Renaissance poets who so describe Michael range in date from about 1550 to 1660, in nationality from Italian to Spanish to German to Dutch to English. Since there is striking similarity in the manner in which they depict the angel Michael as leading personage and antagonist of Lucifer, I refer to the Michael whom they have "collectively" created as the Renaissance Michael. Of the poets I treat, Milton almost certainly knew Valvasone and may have known his own contemporary Vondel, whose reputation was considerable on the continent. It is less certain whether he knew writers like Peri and Taubmann. Watson Kirkconnell, in *The Celestial Cycle* (Toronto, 1952), treats the problem of Milton's knowledge of specific Renaissance poets, as do other writers like Grant McColley, in Paradise Lost, *An Account of its Growth and Major Origins* (Chicago, 1940), and Maury Thibaut de Maisières, in *Les Poèmes inspirés du début de la Genèse à l'époque de la Renaissance* (Louvain, 1931).

6. Garparo Murtola, *Della Creatione del Mondo* (Venice, 1608), canto 1, stanza 64 (p. 22). Alonso de Acevedo, "Dia Primero," *De la Creacion del Mundo,* in *Biblioteca de autores españoles* 29:2 (Madrid, 1864), 250. Whereas, according to Thibaut de Maisières, many sections of Acevedo's poem are plagiarized either from Tasso's *Sette Giornati del Mondo Creato* or from Ferrante Guizone's translation of Du Bartas, the passage describing the war in Heaven is thought to be original. (Thibaut de Maisières, *Poèmes*, pp. 70–71).

7. Friedrich Taubmann, *Bellum Angelicum,* in *Epulum Musaeum* (Leipzig, 1597), p. 87.

in many of these descriptions of Michael, for it is the weapon used frequently to effect Lucifer's defeat. In the dramas, Vondel's *Lucifer* (1654) and Peri's *La Guerra Angelica* (before 1612), there are scenes in which Michael is equipped for battle. Vondel's Michael, for example, hearing that Lucifer has forsaken his vows, calls to his squire to put into his hand God's banner and lightnings.[8] Michael thus has the physical presence of a leader: striking beauty, splendid arms, authority.

This charisma is a quality Milton's Michael has to some degree and his Son of God has in abundance. Michael in *Paradise Lost* is princely, and Milton accords him dignity of place as the leader with Gabriel of the celestial armies. But he is not singled out for physical description and so seems a shade less brilliant than the Renaissance Michael. Instead it is the Son who shines before us "in Celestial Panoply all arm'd / Of radiant *Urim,* work divinely wrought" (VI.761–62). It is he, not Michael, we see armed for battle; assuming God's Bow and Thunder, God's Almighty Arms, girding the Sword upon his "puissant Thigh" (VI.713–14). The Son sets forth in his chariot, bright with the "colors of the show'ry Arch" and set with beryl, crystal, sapphire, and amber. The presence and authority which in the Renaissance poems belong to Michael, in *Paradise Lost* belong to the Son.

One of the reasons for the Renaissance Michael's authority is his intimacy with God. Milton's Michael in Book VI is dispatched from God's throne in a very formal manner, ordered by the Almighty to drive "with Fire and hostile Arms" the godless crew from Heaven. Michael departs with his armed saints, obedient but silent. In corresponding scenes of many Renaissance poems, Michael attains more prominence. God speaks to him directly, not only making him commander of the celestial armies but appointing him warrior to battle personally with Lucifer. And Michael, replying to God's speech, promises his allegiance. In Valvasone's *Angeleida* (1590), for example, Michael proclaims how glorious it is to fight beneath God's standard and swears that he will exact vengeance for God.[9] In Alfano's *La Battaglia Celeste*

---

8. J. V. Vondel, *Lucifer* (Amsterdam, 1654), act 4, sc. 1, pp. 43–44. Translated by Watson Kirkconnell, *The Celestial Cycle,* p. 400.

9. Erasmo de Valvasone, *Angeleida* (Venice, 1590) canto 1, stanzas 121–23, (p. 21).

tra Michele e Lucifero (1568) and Peri's *La Guerra Angelica,*
Michael also responds warmly to God's commands. In giving
Michael supreme command, Peri's God also transfers his own
scepter and power to the loyal archangel, who thus gains eternal
empire over his cruel adversary.[10] Alfano's God makes it explicit
that Michael is leading for him Christ's own army.[11] Milton, who
has not endowed his Michael with so intimate a relationship with
God, so endows his Son. Milton's God confides in the Son, as he
has not in Michael, setting forth his great plan to him. For the
Father has chosen to give the Son the glory of ending the war. To
him then and not to Michael, whom the Renaissance poets had
shown endowed with God's power, Milton's God transfers
authority. The Son responds, as the Renaissance Michael had
done, by giving his pledge of faith and obedience.

> this I my Glory account,
> My exaltation, and my whole delight,
> That thou in me well pleas'd, declar'st thy will
> Fulfill'd . . .
>
> (VI.726–29)[12]

It is natural, of course, that Milton should demonstrate the Son's
intimacy with the Father. And it is significant that this intimacy is
demonstrated on the occasion of the Father's transferring *battle
power* to the Son, for in earlier poems it was Michael so favored
and so praised.

In his confrontations with Lucifer, the Renaissance Michael
also proves a more forceful character than Milton's. Frequently,
in sixteenth- and seventeenth-century poems and dramas, Michael
is given the opportunity to answer Lucifer directly as he first
advances his prideful plans. For example, in Thomas Heywood's
The Hierarchie of the blessed Angels (1635), Michael, upon
hearing Lucifer's boast that he will exalt his throne above God's,
immediately answers:

10. Giovandomenico Peri, *La Guerra Angelica* (ms. Florence: Biblioteca Nazionale),
pp. 84–85. Kirkconnell dates this poem before 1612.

11. Antonino Alfano, *La Battaglia Celeste tra Michele e Lucifero* (Palermo, 1578),
p. 45.

12. Quotations from *Paradise Lost* are cited from John Milton, *Complete Poems and
Major Prose,* ed. Merritt Y. Hughes (New York, 1957).

> Why what is he,
> That like the Lord our God aspires to be?
> In vaine, ô *Lucifer,* thou striv'st t' assay,
> That we thine innovations should obey:
> Who know, as God doth purpose, be, it must;
> He cannot will, but what is good and iust;
> Therefore, with us, that God and Man adore,
> Or in this place thou shalt be found no more.
>
> (p. 340)

In many other poems also, Michael quickly challenges Lucifer's presumption. In Mollerus' *De Creatione et Angelorum Lapsu Carmen* (1596) he indicts Lucifer for his blasphemous words and at the same time attempts to dissuade him from a rebellion that is clearly futile.[13] To revolt from a Creator, who is the source of honor, hope, and safety, he points out, is to revolt from reason itself. Similarly, in Valmarana's *Daemonomachiae,* Michael urges that there is no true honor and good apart from God and demands that Lucifer uphold the faith plighted by him to God as *magister* of Heaven (p. 26). In other scenes as well, Michael appears as the champion of good. In Vondel's *Lucifer,* for example, he upbraids the assembled band of Lucifer's followers, offering on the one hand to mediate any dispute, but warning on the other that violence will be punished. All, he declares, except those who fight under his banner, war against God.[14] Michael in Taubmann's, Valvasone's, and Alfano's poems meets Lucifer on the battlefield and, like a proper classical warrior, exchanges words with him before engaging him in combat. He denounces him as a traitor and demands that he quit Heaven. His words, particularly in Valvasone's poem, closely resemble those of Milton's Michael, who meeting Lucifer before their single duel brands him as the "author of evil" and demands that he leave "Heav'n the seat of bliss" (VI.262–76).[15] Yet even though Milton's Michael in this

13. Fredericus Mollerus, *De Creatione et Angelorum Lapsu Carmen* (Leyden: Thomas Basson, 1596), n.p.

14. Vondel, *Lucifer,* pp. 34–37 (tr. Kirkconnell, *Celestial Cycle,* pp. 392–94).

15. Valvasone, *Angeleida,* canto 2, stanzas 119–20 (p. 43):

Traditor, monstro diuerso . . .	Traitor, strange monster
Di quante sceleragini cosperso	With how many evils have you sprinkled about
Hai d'ognintorno l'infelice busto,	Your unhappy body in every part;

particular episode resembles the Renaissance Michael, his role in *Paradise Lost* as champion of faith is much smaller than was his predecessor's in the Renaissance. For it is not Milton's Michael, but his Abdiel, who first rises to answer Lucifer's charges, to refute his lies, and to decry his presumptuous challenge of God. Further, it is Abdiel who first meets Satan on the battlefield, and adding deeds to words, repulses him with a mighty blow. To the humblest of angels, rather than to the highest, Milton has assigned this role of foremost champion, and in so doing he again parts company with earlier poets who had so characterized Michael.

Throughout Book VI of *Paradise Lost,* Michael, though prominent among the angels, acts a more limited part in the war than does the Michael of Valvasone or Taubmann or Alfano. It is true that he does, as in the Renaissance poems, lead forth his angels, draw the line of battle, bid the martial trumpet sound, and direct the course of battle. But whereas Milton tells us summarily that Michael so acts, other Renaissance poets often describe him in action. And although Milton reports the words of the angel Michael only once, the other poets repeatedly record his speeches. Particularly effective are those speeches in which he encourages his soldiers to enter battle and those in which he presses them on to victory. In *Bellum Angelicum* he appears at the outset of the war, his sword raised in his hand; first he denounces Lucifer's evil and then he urges his angels to the mighty work before them. Let us go, he says, into the frenzy of battle, and though the way is hard, let us not give in to fear and despair. Our commission, he continues, is just and we must execute it with justice. The dragon incites this war, he concludes, but ours is the victory ("hoc Draco dat bellum, nostra est victoria belli").[16] In canto 2 of *Angeleida,* with similar words, Michael in the heat of battle urges his soldiers

---

Di tanti busti ti raddoppia & gira Teco ogni forma di spauento, & d'ira. . . .	With so many bodies every form of terror and wrath redoubles you and turns about you.
Questo albergo è di Dio, questa contrada E di popul, ch'a tui serue, & s'inchina	This dwelling is God's, this country Belongs to people who serve him and bow to him;
Vattene tu co' tuoi seguaci rei . . .	Go hence with your wicked followers.
	(My translation)

16. Taubmann, *Bellum Angelicum*, p. 97.

to pursue the enemy. In true epic style he exhorts them to
remember that they are the noble progeny of God, that they
defend the country in which they were born, and that they are
engaged in the most fitting work they might accomplish. Fight for
Heaven, he cries, and conquer![17]

Clearly, Milton has avoided giving Michael prominence as the
loyal general. Neither before the battle nor during the winning
forays of the first day does he step forward to encourage his
angels. On the second day he is not singled out as an individual
leader, but with his followers first meets defeat from the cannons
and then rises to counterattack by hurling the hills. He acts with
the angels collectively; he is not seen leading them nor is he heard.
In fact, it is during the duel with Satan on the first day that
Michael acts for the last time in Book VI as an individualized
character. Milton has modelled this duel on those which appear in
Renaissance poems before him. Watson Kirkconnell has quite
rightly pointed out the resemblance between the combat of
Michael with Lucifer in *Angeleida* and the combat in *Paradise
Lost*.[18] In *Angeleida,* Lucifer is a Briareus-like giant who wields
weapons in fifty of his hundred arms, ranging the field and up-
setting the angels who oppose him. Yet when he comes to duel
with Michael, he acts much like the classical warrior he is in
Paradise Lost. The duel in *Angeleida* is perfectly patterned on
Homer. Michael first, like Hector or Menelaus, poises his lance
and prays that he may be victorious and raise his enemy's spoil in
Heaven. Next he throws the lance, which pierces the shield and
armor of Lucifer and causes him to retreat. Michael, Achilles-like,
pursues Lucifer, challenges him to single combat, and then draws
his sword and wounds him severely. The wounding, as the sword
pierces through wing and arm and draws forth blood, is described
graphically by Valvasone, as it will be also by Milton.[19] More
briefly, yet still graphically, is this episode recounted by Alfano in
La Battaglia Celeste tra Michele e Lucifero. Michael pursues the
fleeing warrior to challenge him and defeat him with a single
blow.[20] In Acevedo's and Murtola's poems as well, the war draws

17. Valvasone, *Angeleida,* canto 2, stanzas 77–79 (p. 36).
18. Kirkconnell, *Celestial Cycle,* pp. 82–83.
19. Valvasone, *Angeleida,* canto 2, stanzas 116–24 (pp. 42–44).
20. Alfano, *Battaglia Celeste,* pp. 51–52.

to its climax with the sword of Michael victoriously overcoming Lucifer with its single blow.[21] In Peri's *La Guerra Angelica,* the loyal archangel faces more difficulty. He does not simply come and conquer. Lucifer at the end of the war has been metamorphosed into a fire-breathing dragon, who seems almost impervious to attack and who has caused Michael himself momentarily to retreat. The dragon has struck at him with fierce talons, and these blows reverberate throughout Heaven and earth. But Michael at last turns upon the dragon, wounds him, and causes him to flee.[22] In Vondel's *Lucifer* as well, Michael only at last overcomes a dangerous foe. Lucifer is mounted in a chariot drawn by a lion and a dragon, and it is he who seeks out Michael to attack him. He first attempts to cut down God's battle standard and then assaults with his battle axe Michael's adamantine shield. But his battle axe instead shatters. Then Michael, fortified by God's power, raises his hand and strikes Lucifer, not with his sword, but with a thunderbolt. Lucifer is hurled backward from his chariot, and as he falls his standard, the morning star, begins to fade and he himself is transformed into a brutish beast.[23]

Uppermost in the duels of the Renaissance between Michael and Lucifer is the struggle of arms. Michael's victory is attributable, in part, to a sword all but invincible. Moreover, he displays the heroic qualities of superhuman strength and determination with which classical heroes like Achilles and Aeneas were traditionally endowed. Yet, while these qualities are uppermost, the heroic Michael cannot merely be categorized as just another epic strongman. Superior warrior though he is, he is also a spiritual representation of right. He wins the war because right must triumph. And the poets are clear in their responsibility to show a moral as well as a spiritual victory. Michael is, after all, the champion of God's will. In *Angeleida* we see his sunlike brilliance eclipse Lucifer's light. In *Lucifer,* Michael becomes godlike as he turns to face his opponent, shining in arms as though ringed with suns, overcoming by his brilliance the fading morning star. In Heywood's *Hierarchie,* Michael's humility and reverence defeat Lucifer's insolence and spleen, for Heywood insists that the

21. Acevedo, "Dia Primero," p. 250. Murtola, *Della Creatione,* p. 26.
22. Peri, *Guerra Angelica,* p. 112.
23. Vondel, *Lucifer,* pp. 57–60; (tr. Kirkconnell, *Celestial Cycle,* pp. 412–14).

war in Heaven, unlike earthly war, is fought with spiritual rather than material arms: "no Lances, Swords nor Bombards" were employed nor "other Weapons now in use with men." It is a battle in which the expressed power of spiritual goodness triumphs: "Therefore this dreadfull battell fought we finde / By the two motions of the Will and Minde."[24]

Milton has taken an independent attitude toward the part epic *machia,* part *psychomachia,* which earlier poets had delineated. Placing it early in the war on the first day, he has radically changed the nature of the duel by making it inconclusive. No other poet I know of has engaged the loyal archangel in a duel with Satan and then denied him the honor of routing Satan. Though Michael does not fail to wound his adversary, he does fail to check him decisively. Thus Michael's victory, although heroic, becomes ironically no more than the occasion of Satan's temporary discomfiture. And this is still more curious in that Milton has staged a magnificent encounter for the rival angels. Like the Renaissance poets before him, he has made them epic opponents, superhuman adversaries, who meet one another in a contest which seems raised to the highest pitch.

> . . . likest Gods they seem'd,
> Stood they or mov'd, in stature, motion, arms
> Fit to decide the Empire of great Heav'n.
> (VI.301–3)

These "Gods," of course, like Homeric gods or heroes, pit superhuman strength against superhuman strength. We see them wave their fliery swords in the air, their shields like "two broad Suns," blazing opposite. They fight with "next to Almighty Arm." And finally it is the force of Michael's sword, tempered in the Armory of God, which wins the victory. Though undoubtedly this sword-won victory is symbolic of Michael's spiritual preeminence over Satan (the loyal angels war indefatigably on the first day because they are loyal), the contest we see before us is a contest of arms. And the victory that Michael wins has this very limitation, that it is a victory of force over force. Satan thus can renew himself after repulse, and once more armed with physical weaponry challenge the loyal angels, strength against strength.

---

24. Heywood, *Hierarchie,* p. 340.

Michael, Milton seems clearly to say, has with his defence of conventional warfare the means only to hold Satan in stalemate, not to overcome him. As a warrior he is limited.

Thus Milton has turned aside from the kind of warrior the Renaissance Michael was and the kind of duel which he waged. Clearly, he does not wish Michael to meet Satan in a final duel which will afford Satan the opportunity to war with him strength against strength and achieve an heroic if unsuccessful last stand. Earlier Renaissance poets permitted Lucifer to be impressive in his resistance to Michael. Milton, however, is of a different mind. In his account of the war in Heaven, he will provide no grounds for Satan's future boasts that he achieved glory albeit in defeat. Thus, early in the war we may see Satan the epic hero, gnashing his teeth in defeat as he goes down under Michael's sword. In his climactic encounter with the Son, however, he is hero no longer. No monster with a hundred arms seeks the Son in the battlefield; no dragon flames in the night, offering hazard. Never as an epic adversary does Satan stand before the Son.

In the final episodes of Book VI, Milton's emphasis is wholly on the Son. Michael has faded as a significant force in the war; Satan flees with his angels collectively, no single opponent. The Son shines with that charisma and spiritual authority which we saw in Valvasone's or Vondel's Michael. But, as we have also noted, this spiritual authority was sometimes equivocal. Though lit by spirit, the Renaissance Michael behaved like a conventional soldier. In the Son, spirit predominates. The emblems of soldiership are alchemized by the spirit that illuminates them. For the Son, while in many ways acting like an epic hero, is not truly one. Here is no mere Hector, "gloomy as Night," though adorned with Hector's epithet; no heroic boaster, for deeply ironic is his challenge to the rebels that he will try in battle "which the stronger proves, they all / Or I alone against them" (VI.319–20). Impressive though his arms may be, his bow and quiver and three-bolted lightning, these are not conventional weapons for offense or defense, but symbols of power and energy. Nor does he draw and use his sword, the weapon which had been inseparable from Michael. His breastplate, adorned with the Urim, is no battle hero's, but the priest's. And his chariot, which Satan tried vainly to imitate with his flaming cherubim and golden shields, is more than sun-bright; it is, itself, instinct with spirit, the living emblem that his victory is not of arms but of himself. The Son does not win a battle waged by courage and strength. Such force as he uses is checked at half strength, for he encourages no contest. Indeed no contest is possible. The purpose of his warfare is to repudiate force by force, to demonstrate how vain warfaring strength is to those who "by strength . . . measure all, of other excellence / Not emulous" (VI.820–22). Nor does he strive for glory, which Satan had appointed the utmost aim of warfaring. The Son's glory is not attendant upon any feat of arms. Antecedent to, rather than the result or reward of, battle, it shines before him, restoring heavenly order, inspiring the angels to quiet joy and the rebels to grief. It is the cause, not the effect, of his victory, for at the sight of his glory the rebels are overcome.

In the victory that follows, moreover, the Son, as he returns to God's throne, displays his spiritual authority, restoring Heaven to peace and order on the one hand and to unanimity on the other. Milton here is indebted once more to the Renaissance poems before him, for many of them include lavish descriptions of the ceremonial return of the victorious Michael to God. In these victory scenes, as in the duel that preceded them, Michael acts a double role, part conquering general, part saint. On the one hand, the poets are rhapsodic about the spiritual victory. In *Angeleida,* heavenly flowers bloom, filling the air with delicious odors; in Murtola's *Della Creatione del Mondo,* an account where the descriptions of the aftermath of the war are lengthier by far than those of the preceding action, Heaven shines resplendently. In *La Guerra Angelica,* Michael, presenting himself at God's throne, is proclaimed God's minister and given authority over the lucent spheres of Heaven.[25] Yet even as the poets celebrate the superb spiritual victory of this greatest of angels, we are unmistakably reminded of a pomp that is military in its overtones. What we see in fact is a Roman triumph. Trumpets sound, palms are waved, the loyal angels march like well-drilled classical soldiers. Earthly comparisons abound, though raised to heavenly superlatives. The pomp in Heaven is compared with that of France and Rome, and Michael, welcomed as the greatest of heroes, is said to surpass

25. Valvasone, *Angeleida,* canto 3, stanza 57 (p. 55); Murtola, *Della Creatione,* stanzas 77–103 (pp. 27–35). Peri, *Guerra Angelica,* pp. 113–14.

those earthly generals who reward their soldiers with gold and silver.[26] Once more his formidable armor is described, once more his invincible sword raised before us. The choruses of angels which ring out to greet this warrior praise the force of his arm which effected Lucifer's defeat.[27] He himself delivers victory speeches wherein he exults in his conquest of the archfiend. In Peri's play, he presents his trophies to God in evidence that he has overcome his rival. The commendatory sonnet with which Valvasone ends his epic celebrates a martial victor.

Eccelso Heroe	Highest hero,
Campion invitto & Santo	Invincible champion and saint
De l'impero diuin, per cui pigliasti	Of the divine empire, for which
L'alta contesa, e'l reo Dragon caciasti	You have fought the high contest,
De l'auree stelle deballato, & franto . . .	And have chased the wicked dragon
	From the golden stars, subdued and
	crushed . . .[28]

In these final proceedings, Michael the general outshines Michael the saint, force outweighs faith.

Milton's celebrations for the Son, like in kind to those of the Renaissance poems, are wholly different in intent. Milton waves no palms for military victory. He celebrates neither the force of his warring Son, nor that of the angels who warred before him. The palms waved for his returning Son do not look to a Roman victory, but look beyond to the brief triumph he will enjoy as king incarnate entering Jerusalem and the more joyous triumph as king victorious, resurrected and reentering Heaven. With the Son's

26. Murtola, *Della Creatione,* stanza 83 (p. 29).
27. See Peri, *Guerra Angelica,* act. 5, sc. 2:

O glorioso Duce,	O glorious leader,
O celeste Guerriero,	O celestial warrior,
C'ha troui al fier Dragon l'empio	Who has discovered the impious thought
pensiero.	of the proud dragon.
	(My translation)

See also Vondel, *Lucifer,* Act 5:

Gezegent zy de Helt,	Blest be that hero most,
Die't goddeloos gewelt;	Who all the godless host,
En zijn maght, en zijn kracht,	With standard and with power
en zijn standert	and with might
Ter neder heeft gevelt,	Hath cast down from their boast.
(Vondel, p. 61)	(Kirkconnell, p. 416)

28. Valvasone, *Angeleida,* p. 63 (my translation).

victory over Satan in *Paradise Lost,* Milton is not concerned with
a military achievement. We see in the Son the true king who has
purged Heaven of the ruinous assault Satan has raised and
restored it to peace and joy. What we see in his return to God is
his resumption of his true place in Heaven, which will assure the
continuance of that peace and joy. In Michael's return, the
Renaissance poets irresistibly celebrate the heroic deed as well as
the person. In the Son, the person shines supreme.

Thus Milton, though decisively influenced by those poems in
which Michael appears as hero of the war in Heaven, takes an
independent way in depicting both his own Michael and his own
Son. Milton has accorded to Michael the same place as the
Renaissance poets did, as leader of the angels; but he has sharply
restricted Michael's achievements both as military and spiritual
leader. He has permitted him fine moments; but he never permits
him to become the transcendent figure that the Renaissance
Michael so often is. Transcendent, of course, is precisely what the
Son in *Paradise Lost* is, assuming command when Michael and his
angels become deadlocked against Satan, but becoming more than
champion and general. Like the Renaissance Michael, however,
the Son is an agent personally selected by God. Unswerving in his
purpose, he comes to fulfill God's will. In tones that recall the
Renaissance Michael's denunciation of Satan, the Son convicts the
rebels of their wickedness and asserts God's right over them.

> . . . of this cursed crew
> The punishment to other hand belongs;
> Vengeance is his, or whose he sole appoints;
> (VI.806–8)

That he here serves as God's agent, rather than as God Himself
(from whom in the Creation sequence that follows he is barely
distinguished), is significant. Milton always had the option of
ending the war in Heaven with the direct intervention of God. So
medieval accounts and not a few Renaissance poets (see Spenser
and Naogeorgus, for example) had allowed.[29] God with his
lightning or, as Spenser relates, by his mighty breath expels

29. See Spenser, *The Hymne of Heavenly Love* (ll. 85–88); Thomas Naogeorgus
(Thomas Kirchmeyer), "Satyrarum liber primus," in *Delitiae poetarum germanorum,* ed.
Gruterus (Frankfurt, 1612), IV, 1060.

Lucifer from Heaven. But Milton does not follow this tradition. It is the Son as the willing agent of God, choosing to serve the Father Satan has denied, who brings the war to a close. Milton thus has retained for the Son what had been the heart of Michael's role in the Renaissance epics and dramas: that of loyal servant. Of course, for the Son servanthood has wider applications. His is not so much the soldierly discipline manifest in the Renaissance Michael but perfect obedience to be further exercised as he becomes the second Adam. His is more than angelic zeal, but selfless desire (as we see in Book III as well) to sacrifice all, that God's will might be done. And as he arrives at the end of Book VI in his splendid chariot, his coming is more than that of an invincible military leader. It is also emblematic of future comings: the judgment and comforting of the fallen Adam and Eve, the destruction of Sin and Death and the redemption of man, and finally the binding of Satan and inauguration at the final age of peace on earth, as now in Heaven. As he dresses the Son in the armor and equipage which in earlier poems had adorned the angel Michael and as he commissions him to end the war, Milton presents for us a hero whose deeds and victory are above heroic.

The Hero of Paradise Lost
One More Time

JOHN T. SHAWCROSS

So much has been written about the hero of *Paradise Lost* that another statement about that topic may seem unwarranted. But I see the question a bit differently from the way it has been attacked in the past: criticism of the poem has moved beyond the kinds of formulations we learned in graduate schools in recent years. Milton's execution of the hero, a staple of epic, depends, of course, on the epic's thesis, its theme, and its genre, as well as its mode. I have previously argued that the thesis is that Eternal Providence can be asserted to Man, thereby justifying God's ways; that the theme is love; that the genre is epic but that the mode is comedic.[1] The question concerning the hero is really various questions: Is there a hero in the poem? If there is, who is the hero? If there is no hero, how does one view Satan? and the basic question, What does one mean by hero? Milton himself called his poem a "Heroic Song" (IX.25).[2] The existence of a hero in *Paradise Lost* has always been assumed, it seems, although Addison at one point states there is no hero, in contradiction to Dryden's candidacy of Satan, but then he argues that the Son

1. See John T. Shawcross, "The Son in His Ascendance: A Reading of *Paradise Lost*," *Modern Language Quarterly*, 27 (1966) 388–401; "The Style and Genre of *Paradise Lost*" in *New Essays on* Paradise Lost, ed. Thomas Kranidas (Berkeley: Univ. of California Press, 1969), pp. 15–33; and "The Balanced Structure of *Paradise Lost*," *Studies in Philology*, 62 (1965) 696–718.

2. All quotations are from my edition of *The Complete Poetry of John Milton* (Garden City: Anchor Books, 1971).

would be more likely if a hero must be advanced.[3] Probably the classification of the poem as epic has led to the assumption, and certainly its being viewed as tragedy has. But if the poem falls under the comedic mode, then the stature of the hero must be different: the hero would not necessarily be one of noble rank, fighting to overcome injustice and succumbing in the process, and his action and achievement need not be exemplary.

In a concept of tragedy Satan is hero only if one believes that God has been and is wrong in his treatment of the angels and particularly of Satan, and perhaps in His ways toward man. The "heroic" Satan, who, it is argued, undergoes change from glorious figure in Books I and II to despicable devil with his soliloquy in Book IV, still blights Milton criticism.[4] First, Satan is hardly heroic in Books I and II when one reads carefully: he lies, deceives himself and others, boasts without foundation, aggrandizes himself, sets up situations to promote himself like any con man of the daily tabloids. His exciting speeches and rhetorical arts have won over readers as well as the imaginary auditors. But second, and even more important because we are immediately thrust back in time to the condition leading to the war in heaven and forward in the poem itself, although we do not then realize it, is Satan's doing that of which he accuses God: assuming superiority and leadership over others who thereby become inferiors and followers. There is hierarchy in heaven and Satan acknowledges that hierarchy approvingly according to the earlier parts of Raphael's account in Book V. But the "begetting" of a being to whom Satan is ranked "inferior" and "follower" causes him to rebel against God, not very logically but with great psychological validity. First, he objects to that which he himself asserts and in Books I and II demands of his cohorts. Second, he acts out of pride and envy, without allowing others (God or his followers) to exercise their own unconditional or unconditioned decisions. And

3. "The *Paradise Lost* is an Epic, or a Narrative Poem, and he that looks for an Hero in it, searches for that which *Milton* never intended; but if he will needs fix the Name of an Hero upon any Person in it, 'tis certainly the *Messiah* who is the Hero, both in the Principal Action, and in the Chief Episodes," *The Spectator*, No. 297 (9 Feb. 1712). For John Dryden's remark see, "Dedication of the Aeneis," *The Works of Virgil* (London, 1697), p. 180.

4. See, for example, Frank S. Kastor, "Milton's Tempter: A Genesis of a Subportrait in *Paradise Lost*," *Huntington Library Quarterly* 33 (1970), 373–85.

third, like too many critics, Satan forgets that the Son is God[5] and that the "begetting" of the Son is not suddenly introducing someone new who is superior to Satan, but rather establishing an administration in heaven. (The Son is, rather, part of the great Providence of God, who has total prescience.) The Son is still God, and Satan's reaction is the result of an awakening to the fact that he has as high a position as he will ever have in heaven.

One of the paradoxes of life that *Paradise Lost* adumbrates is that nonchange involving the present is an unacceptable concept to most minds, who nonetheless strive to achieve non-changingness for themselves and their associates in the future. While Satan cannot accept the status quo of his life in heaven any more than Adam and Eve through deception can accept the status quo of their Edenic life, he still seeks a world of stasis after his fall: "A mind not to be chang'd by Place or Time" (I.253), a "Divided Empire with Heav'ns King" (IV.111). This is the fascistic lure of all Republics or Utopias or New Harmonys or conforming nonconformists. The fullest literary answer to this paradox is Joyce's in *Ulysses* and more obviously in *Finnegans Wake*: all of you who have fallen, wake up; accept life as it is in all its goodness and all its evil and all its being. Surely Bloom and Earwicker are the prime examples in literature of the antithesis to the antihero.

Satan is willing to accept, it seems, a position under God and over other angels (it is unclear whether Michael and others have equivalent positions) until God's generation into Father and Son underscores Satan's lesser position to God. This aspect of Satan's being is just as evident in Books I and II as it is in Books V and VI. Why else advancement of "revenge," "immortal hate" (a static condition), "courage never to submit or yield," "A mind not to be chang'd by Place or Time," the emphasis on reigning even though in Hell, the opening of Book II with Satan splendiferously set on a throne with the other fallen angels below him, looking up? Milton has not given us two different Satans in *Paradise Lost,* one in Books I and II and another from Book IV on; what he has done is

---

5. Perhaps this begs the question of Milton's alleged anti-trinitarianism. There is nothing in *Paradise Lost* which denies divinity to the Son. He does not exhibit omnipresence (except as agent for the Father), omniscience, or omnipotence (except again as agent for the Father), but this does not state a so-called Arian position; rather it indicates Milton's adherence to a common nonheretical doctrine known as subordinationism.

make emphatically clear that such matters are in the eye of the beholder. Milton has not really tried to mislead, either, for the simile of the bees is clearly intended to show that these superheroic statures of Book I are but swarms of buzzing little drones, superheroic only in their own eyes. The simile of the "Pigmean Race" or "Faerie Elves" repeats the message, the narrative voice remarking, "they but now who seem'd / In bigness to surpass Earths Giant Sons / Now less than smallest Dwarfs" (I.777–79).

Probably Milton thought that his epic showed that God had not been wrong in his ways toward Satan: it was his aim to justify the ways of God toward men. He did not anticipate rejection of God though he recognized the need to make the rules of God's world acceptable to man. If God has not been wrong in his ways toward Satan, then Satan cannot be a hero driving out injustice. If Milton succeeds in justifying God's ways toward men, as I think he does and have previously argued,[6] then man (Adam and Eve, or Mankind) does not function as hero in the usual sense of the word for a piece of literature controlled by the tragic mode. And Adam shows none of the epic hero qualities that we have come to expect from works like the *Aeneid*. Adam is progenitor, but further likenesses to an Aeneas lie in material not included in the poem and occurring after the final lines. In the story of Adam and Eve we have the potentialities of the common heroic figure: either one who falls through some *hamartia,* which he must overcome to achieve a new balance in his world, previously unbalanced through evil or injustice or his own excess or misjudgment, or one who founds a new world to reject the past and develop a glorious future.

The way we should view Satan is as the prototype antihero and Adam and Eve as the protagonist in the drama of life (a kind of morality piece). The antihero is one who, unlike Bloom or Earwicker, does not accept life as it is, things as they are, but who tries against incalculable odds to change the makeup of the world and his puny position in it. An antihero is not simply a nonhero or one opposed to the hero; he is a specific personality type, explainable in psychological terms. Dostoievsky's "underground man" notes that "the whole work of man really seems to consist in nothing but proving to himself every minute that he is a man and

6. See "The Son in His Ascendance" cited in n. 1 above.

not a piano-key!"; the constant change sought he expresses thus: "perhaps the only goal on earth to which mankind is striving lies in this incessant process of attaining, in other words, in life itself, and not in the thing to be attained." Like Satan he reasons in extreme alternatives only: "Either to be a hero or to grovel in the mud—there was nothing between. That was my ruin, for when I was in the mud I comforted myself with the thought that at other times I was a hero, and the hero was a cloak for the mud: for an ordinary man it was shameful to defile himself, but a hero was too lofty to be utterly defiled, and so he might defile himself."[7] This sounds like Milton's Satan in the first book in Hell, talking of his glorious past, so oblivious to the horrors of "immortal hate" and the self-condemnation in arguing that "who overcomes / By force, hath overcome but half his foe" (I.648–49). His lack of acceptance of things as they are can be seen when he criticizes God as thinking He reigns securely on His throne because of "old repute, / Consent or custom" (I.639–40), which is Satan's own goal, we know. The antihero laments rank in the world and his insectlike condition, but, paradoxically, it is not a thoroughgoing democratic world he seeks. At the base of Dostoievsky's protagonist's psychology is death wish ("Perhaps suffering is just as great a benefit to him as well-being? Man is sometimes extraordinarily, passionately, in love with suffering, and that is a fact"),[8] just as it is the driving force in Satan's personality. Satan's bent toward uncreation cannot possibly accord with the positiveness that heroic action demands. The antihero bemoans his existence because others have more power, more beauty, more talent, and so forth; he hates himself ultimately and thus envies those around him. Can his first view of Adam and Eve be any other way interpreted?

> O Hell! what doe mine eyes with grief behold,
> Into our room of bliss thus high advanc't
> Creatures of other mould, earth-born perhaps,
> Not Spirits, yet to heav'nly Spirits bright
> Little inferior . . .
>
> (IV.358–62)

7. Constance Garnett's translation of *Notes from Underground* in Notes from Underground, Poor People, The Friend of the Family, *3 Short Novels by Fyodor Dostoyevsky* (New York: Dell, 1960), pp. 51, 52, 73, respectively.

8. Ibid., p. 53.

But no one could possibly believe that Milton is condemning action to correct the evils and injustices of this world. The antihero is not the hero, yet that confusion is the cause for the controversy over Satan and the detraction heaped on Milton as artist.

In *The Tenure of Kings and Magistrates* Milton made quite clear the difference between the true David and the false David, for Charles I was heralded as a David by the Royalists, and his main line of argument is that when the power of kings and magistrates, which has been conferred upon them by the people in covenant for common peace and benefit, has been abused, it is the people's duty to reassume that power or to alter it in whatever way is most conducive to the public good. Satan and God pose a question almost impossible of answer until after the fact or by faith: Who is the true God or leader? The portrait of Satan in Books I and II, as elsewhere, etches his falsity and duplicity, envy and egocentricity. He is neither God nor true leader, but rather the antitype of Corah, rebel against Moses, and thus antithesis of Moses. He would lead men into the bondage of Pharaoh (who is identified with Satan himself). Milton's Satan does not really allow us to misjudge whether he is true or leader. And much as some modern critics dislike Milton's God and the way that the theology he supports operates, the person of God, Father and Son and Spirit, that appears in *Paradise Lost* is the person of a true God and a true fountainhead of life. If one wants to argue with religion, that is one thing, but literature which makes use of that philosophy is another.

The action to recover the people from the false kings and magistrates and to achieve the new commonweal is heroic and takes a hero to accomplish. It should be undertaken as the mid-century movement against the monarchy of the Stuarts attempted to reclaim the natural rights of man. Such a hero was not one who thought of himself as insect, who primarily wished position and acclaim for himself, who tried to change the world because of himself; he was one who thought of himself as an image of God, who aimed at the general good, and who deprecated the conditions of man's life (not man's fate), devolved to its present state through man's avarice and the like. It is the confounding of the antiheroic Satan with the heroic-sounding lines he often speaks which has caused some to place Milton in Satan's camp. In a world of thwarted causes (the end of the eighteenth century or the 1960s and 70s) it is easy to read hope into "What though the field be lost? / All is not lost"; or even "courage never to submit or yield"; or even perhaps, in the most depressed moments, "Better to reign in Hell, then serve in Heav'n" if Heaven is a middle-class 1930 Hollywood-like existence in a middle-class Norman-Vincent-Peale-like mind. Milton, I have no doubt whatsoever, would heartily approve and join those of the late eighteenth century or 1960s or 70s who had the courage not to submit and not to give up hope and to live in the ghetto rather than on Elm Street near Winding Lane. Indeed it is this quality of Milton's mind—and it comes through in so many works in addition to *Paradise Lost*—that has attracted the rebels of this world. But in the poem it is Satan who says these things against God (a symbol at least of perfection), and who follows them with repugnant concepts: "unconquerable Will" (even when proved wrong?), "study of revenge," "immortal hate," and the most horrendous of all, "A mind not to be chang'd by Place or Time."

Milton's aim in *Paradise Lost* is to achieve a spectrum of heroic action and its antitheses as just outlined. In Satan we have the antithesis of heroic action although he appropriates the language of that action. That some continue to be won over by Satan's arts of rhetoric either commends Milton's artistry or condemns those readers' ability to read and evaluate. In the Son are oppositions of purpose, achievement, and goals. The Son represents the doer of God's commands, not only in the defeat of Satan in the war in heaven, or in the creation, or in the judgment, but also in his role as Man-God toward which Books XI and XII move and in his further role as Judge at the end of time. He becomes the exemplary hero, or prototype hero, for all men. Rather than death wish, his drive is love and creation. Since it is the Christ legend which subtends the folkloristic definition of hero described by Lord Raglan in *The Hero: A Study in Tradition, Myth, and Drama,* the Son and not Satan can be seen to function as this form of hero in the poem. Yet the Son is not the hero of *Paradise Lost* in the sense of being the central character of the work or the one to whom Milton has directed his energies, although he appears prominently in Books III, V, VI, VII–VIII (in the person of God),

X, XI, and XII (as Man-God). (We should note that Satan's appearances are not in every book either, and Adam and Eve are prominent in only eight books.) As prototype hero the Son does, however, manifest elements which will appear in the "hero" of the poem.

Adam and Eve, as I have already suggested, constitute the protagonist of the poem in the same way that Everyman is protagonist in the morality play. They are buffeted by the antitheses of Satan and God, that is, by the qualities exemplified by the Son. They are the central characters—or rather, "hand in hand," they constitute the central character—about whom the action revolves. They do not, I believe, function as "hero" in the usual sense of "doer" or exemplar of achievement;[9] they are one who plays out a part against great life forces and they are the example of what life encompasses. Neither are they an antihero like Satan, fighting against those forces, although they are affected by and indicate that Mankind embraces the qualities which give rise to heroism. Their descendants in Books XI and XII illustrate the spectrum of antihero through all grades of hero which exist in the potential of Man. Rather than being folk hero, Adam and Eve represent the archetypal elements of the outcast, banished from the world of Eden for their crime against future man, becoming the wanderer until such time as expiation be totally won:

> The World was all before them, where to choose
> Thir place of rest, and Providence thir guide:
> They hand in hand with wandring steps and slow,
> Through *Eden* took thir solitarie way.
>   (XII.646–49)

For Milton's "hero" we must turn to his remarks in the proem to Book IX.

9. See Peter Hägin's *The Epic Hero and the Decline of Heroic Poetry: A Study of the Neoclassical English Epic with Special Reference to Milton's* Paradise Lost (Bern, 1964), Ch. 5, pp. 146–69, for a discussion of Adam and Eve as hero. Hägin's view and mine are complementary, although I feel he does not push far enough in defining the hero of the poem. The thesis of the study—that the nature of the hero of *Paradise Lost* was a major cause for the decline of the epic—is, I believe, well founded. Sir Richard Blackmore argued in "An Essay on the Nature and Constitution of Epick Poetry" in *Essays upon Several Subjects* (London, 1716), I, 51–52, that the hero must have been Adam himself. His comments dispel the notion confounding the political hero and the moral one.

The comedic mode of *Paradise Lost* demands an ending in hope and joy; the only way in which the lost Eden will be regained is by complete realization

> that to obey is best,
> And love with fear the only God, to walk
> As in his presence, ever to observe
> His providence, and on him sole depend,
> Mercifull over all his works, with good
> Still overcoming evil, and by small
> Accomplishing great things, by things deemd weak
> Subverting worldly strong, and worldly wise
> By simply meek; that suffering for Truths sake
> Is fortitude to highest victorie,
> And to the faithful Death the Gate of Life;
> Taught this by his example whom I now
> Acknowledge my Redeemer ever blest.
> (XII.561–73)

The path is laid out: obedience, love, acceptance of Providence, fortitude (which implies patience toward suffering when such suffering is for Truth, that is, God), and following the example of the Son by obedience, love, fortitude, small deeds, and meekness. By adding faith, virtue, patience, temperance, charity (XII.581–85) will the happier internal Paradise be found. Clearly Adam is counseled not to pursue the antiheroic life and is counseled toward the heroic life which has been delineated by the actions of the Son. Satan and the Son offer archetypal views of these life-styles, and man will vacillate between them till the end of the world. The comedic mode is sustained by the hope that some will follow the path, for Adam has understood and so may others.

The proem to Book IX reviews these ideas of "heroism" and allows us to conclude that what justly gives heroic name to person (or to poem) is striving valiantly for good against opposing forces. When such forces of good and evil are archetypal or mythic, as within *Paradise Lost,* we have the root and prototype of all heroism. Milton says that his argument is not less but more heroic than Achilles' wrath or Turnus' rage. The heroism displayed in the *Iliad* or the *Aeneid* centers first on war ("hitherto the only

Argument / Heroic deem'd") rather than on love and charity, and second on trappings of feigned actions like jousts and splendid feasts. The heroism Milton chooses to depict is based on patience and martyrdom and is not fabled or feigned, since it represents the truth which he interprets from the Bible. Milton's subject to achieve the name heroic for his poem must be

> foul distrust, and breach
> Disloyal on the part of Man, revolt,
> And disobedience: On the part of Heav'n
> Now alienated, distance and distaste,
> Anger and just rebuke and judgement giv'n,
> That brought into this World a world of woe,
> Sin and her shadow Death, and Miserie
> Deaths Harbinger . . .
>   (IX.6–13)

His higher argument, which is sufficient in itself to grant the name heroic, remains untouched by other writers, and "this great Argument," as the proem to Book I relates, is that the lost seat of Eden will be regained through the action of the Son and through the brooding of dovelike creatures from the abyss within man. This argument had not yet been attempted in prose or rhyme. Heroic action is thus patience (which is action to Milton and not inaction; it equates "stand" as in the last line of his well-known sonnet and in the final action of the Son in *Paradise Regain'd*), sacrifice of self for the love of mankind, and opposition to the forces of evil which surround man and are within man. The name "hero" is justly used for that person who exhibits the better fortitude. The hero of *Paradise Lost* is thus not just an ordinary hero of literature, not a specific personage within the work, but rather every man who follows the path, who learns like Adam the sum of wisdom. His action is personal, significant for him alone, not exemplary, although he may, of course, become a type of Christ *figura* for the mundane mind of man to follow. Although heroic action may also lead others out of bondage through the reestablishment of a new commonweal, it is the heroic action within the self that Milton is concerned with in *Paradise Lost*. Like Gerrard Winstanley and the Diggers, Milton aimed at the improvement of all mankind through the improvement of each man individually, an unstated (perhaps unrealized) goal of recent generations. The truly heroic, Milton urges, will result from the rejection of the elements of antiheroism within man and the pursuit of the "fairer Paradise" by "vanquishing / Temptation" (*PR* IV.613, 607–8). The hero of *Paradise Lost* is the fit audience; the hero may be you.

Index

Abdiel: champion of faith, 127

Acevedo, Alonso de: glorifies Michael, 123, 128–29

Adam and Eve: protagonist of *Paradise Lost,* 144

Addison, Joseph: on the Son as hero of *Paradise Lost,* 137–38

Aeneid: theme of, contrasted to Milton's, 78, 137, 140, 145

Alfano, Antonino: version of Michael versus Lucifer, 124–25, 128

Ambrose, Saint: sermons, 4

Angels: names used by Milton, 28–29; source for Azazel, 26–27; sensuality of Belial, 29; source for Uriel, 29; Raphael's sociability and association with right reason, 29–30; Hebrew signification of Michael, 122. *See also* Michael

Antihero: distinguished from epic hero, 140–42

Apocrypha: defined, 23, 24–25; influence on Milton, 23–43; Miltonic source in, 24, 28; distinguished from Pseudepigrapha, 25–26; rejected by Calvinists, 27; combines Greek and Hebrew thought, 27, 36, 39; doctrinal differences from canonical Bible, 28; on pre-Fall man's immortality, 36–37; combines Hebraic and Platonic thought, 37

Areopagitica: implies truth's many forms, 7; on biblical quotations from pagan poets, 7–8; serious undertone of, in ironic treatment of censoring music, 98

Art, Milton's. *See* Creative process; Inspiration; Muse, Milton's; Poetry

Asmodeus: contrasted with Raphael, 29; equated with lust, 29

Attendant Spirit: related to muse and Wisdom, 37; as genius, both reliable "porter" and true poet, 54–57

Azazel. *See* Angels

Baldwin, Edward Chauncey, 26

Ballard, George: on spiritual effectiveness of poetry, 16

Baroque art: virtuosity in, 109–10

Baroway, Israel: on biblical poetry, 14*n*

Basil, Saint: on spiritual uses of pagan poetry, 8

Belial. *See* Angels

Bernini, Gian Lorenzo: baroque virtuosity of, 109

Beum, Robert T.: on rimes in *Samson Agonistes,* 106

Bible: Milton's use of, for poetry, ix–xiii, 122; rhetorical excellence of, 4; devotional and literary approaches to, 4–5; place of, in education, 13–14; poetry of, 14; as not antithetical to the classics, 18; Geneva version of, 27. *See also* Apocrypha

"Bible as literature": history of the term, 3–4

Boyd, Zachary: versifies Scripture, xi

Broadbent, J. B., 50*n*

Buss, Martin J.; on biblical genres, 4 and *n*

Caccini, Giulio: on words for songs, 89

Calvin, John: favors literal reading of Bible, 4–5; attitude toward Apocrypha, 32 and *n*; distinguishes sacred and human literature, 32–33

COMPOSED BY FOX VALLEY TYPESETTING, MENASHA, WISCONSIN
MANUFACTURED BY CUSHING MALLOY, INC., ANN ARBOR, MICHIGAN
TEXT AND DISPLAY LINES ARE SET IN SABON

Library of Congress Cataloging in Publication Data
Main entry under title:
Milton & the art of sacred song.
Includes bibliographical references and index.
1. Milton, John, 1608–1674—Criticism and
interpretation—Addresses, essays, lectures.
I. Patrick, John Max, 1911– II. Sundell, Roger H.
PR3588.M475   821′.4   78-65014
ISBN 0–299–07830–2